Advance Praise

"*Connected Culture* speaks directly to the real challenge leaders face today: not wanting a better culture in theory, but knowing how to build one in practice. Jamie Shapiro cuts through the noise with a grounded, human approach that shows how trust and connection are shaped through everyday leadership choices. This is a thoughtful, steady guide for leaders who want cultures that truly last—not just ones that sound good."

—**DR. MARSHALL GOLDSMITH,** Thinkers50 #1 Executive Coach and *New York Times* bestselling author of *The Earned Life*, *Triggers*, and *What Got You Here Won't Get You There*

"In *Connected Culture*, Jamie Shapiro blends solid organizational research with clear, actionable steps, showing leaders how to strengthen trust, clarity, and collaboration in their teams."

—**DAN HEATH,** *New York Times* bestselling author of *Reset* and coauthor of *Upstream* and *Switch*

"Every page of *Connected Culture* radiates Jamie's rare combination of clarity, warmth, and wisdom. She brings a deeply human voice to the science of leadership—making complex ideas feel intimate, actionable, and profound. This book doesn't just inform; it resonates. It's the kind of guide you return to again and again, not just for what it says, but for how it makes you feel about the work you do and the people you lead."

—**HELEN GIZA,** CEO, Fresenius Medical Care

"*Connected Culture* offers a powerful reminder: Thriving organizations are built from the inside out. Jamie Shapiro gives leaders the tools to transform connection into performance—with heart, science, and soul."

—**TALIA FOX,** CEO, Kusi Global Inc. and author of *The Power of Conscious Connection*

"What sets Jamie apart is how she blends rigorous science with a truly human touch. Having worked with her for many years, I've seen how deeply her advice is rooted in research-based organizational psychology and neuroscience. She has a rare ability to quickly read team dynamics and open leaders up to growth in a way that feels authentic, practical, and personal. In *Connected Culture*, she distills her approach through the 5Cs framework, turning science and human connection into an essential toolkit for CEOs."

—**MOSTAFA KAMAL,** President and Chief Executive Officer, Prime Therapeutics

"*Connected Culture* is one of the most valuable evidence-informed practical books ever written on how to build thriving teams and organizations. Dr. Jamie Shapiro succeeds where many leadership books fall short—she translates high-quality science into a clear, measurable, and actionable framework that leaders can actually use. The 5Cs Model is elegant, evidence-informed, and deeply human, capturing the core drivers of sustained performance, well-being, and human and organizational flourishing. This book should be required reading for executives and all leaders serious about culture change that truly lasts."

—**STEWART I. DONALDSON, PhD,** Distinguished University Professor, Claremont Graduate University

"In *Connected Culture,* Shapiro distills years of leadership wisdom into a clear framework for leaders who understand that culture is the true competitive advantage. This isn't just theory—it's a practical road map for executives who want to unlock performance by building organizations where people feel both seen and empowered. Insightful and actionable, it's a must-read for anyone committed to building thriving teams, making it essential for leaders at every level."

—**PABLO VEGAS,** CEO, ERCOT

"A must-read for every person who is responsible for and/or contributes to high-performing teams and building company cultures. Cultures tend to happen by default. This book will guide you through how to craft or recalibrate your company's culture with intention: to design one that elevates the company's mission and vision and creates teams of people who become your biggest assets (rather than your biggest liabilities), so that your company can live out its purpose while enjoying the process."

—**DARRAH BRUSTEIN,** Writer, founder, thought leader, and executive coach

"*Connected Culture* is a superb, beautifully written contribution. Shapiro blends credible research, practical frameworks, and vivid personal examples into a model that makes complex issues clear and actionable. A truly valuable resource for leaders and teams."

—**DR. KIM CAMERON,** Professor Emeritus, University of Michigan and pioneering cofounder, Positive Organizational Scholarship

"*Connected Culture* is truly 100% on point. Jamie Shapiro has put into words what so many teams and leaders experience but struggle to articulate and solve. This book provides actionable tools and practical guidance that leaders can immediately put into practice to strengthen communication, trust, and collaboration within their teams. It reflects a deep understanding of how teams actually work—rooted in science, yet tangibly aligned with the realities of human behavior in the workplace.

The 5Cs gave me and my leadership team a shared language for understanding what's happening beneath the surface and a clear, disciplined framework for addressing it together. *Connected Culture* doesn't just identify issues; it leads teams to tangible solutions. This is a must-read for any leader committed to building a trust based, transparent, and thriving organization."

—**JULIE TSCHIDA BROWN,** Chief People and Culture Officer, Zayo

"Jamie Shapiro is a true expert in building culture that works in real teams. *Connected Culture* goes beyond theory, offering an elegant, research-backed framework with practical guidance leaders can rely on for real impact. (Concepts like Candid Communication help teams get to the heart of the behaviors that ignite collaboration and drive performance.) Having had the privilege of working with Jamie, I've seen her recommendations transform teams. And when she says she's got you, she absolutely delivers."

—**JENNIFER LEUER,** CEO and board member

"*Connected Culture* is a needed shift in how we think about performance. With clarity, empathy, and immediate practicality, Jamie Shapiro shows that teams truly thrive when people feel connected, trusted, and able to contribute to something that matters. This is an essential read for all leaders today."

—**ZACH MERCURIO,** PhD, Author of *The Power of Mattering* and *The Invisible Leader*

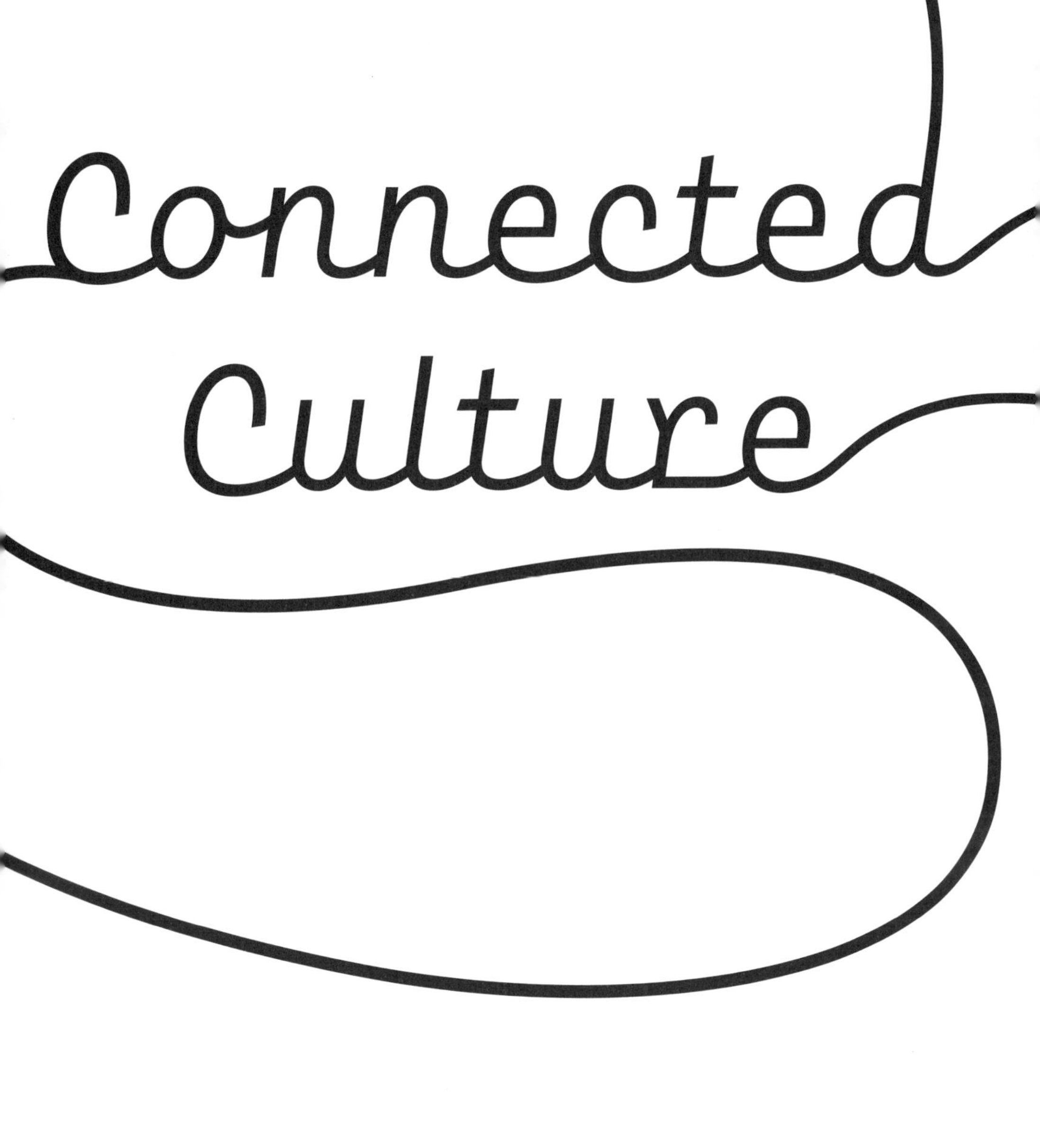
Connected
Culture

Connected Culture

THE NEW SCIENCE FOR THRIVING TEAMS AND CULTURES

Jamie Shapiro

IDEAPRESS PUBLISHING
WASHINGTON, DC

Ideapress Publishing | www.ideapresspublishing.com

Cover Design: Catherine Casalino
Interior Design: Jessica Angerstein

Cataloging-in-Publication Data is on file with the Library of Congress.

Hardcover ISBN: 978-1-64687-234-3

Special Sales
Ideapress books are available at a special discount for bulk purchases for sales promotions and premiums, or for use in corporate training programs. Special editions, including personalized covers, a custom foreword, corporate imprints, and bonus content, are also available.

1 2 3 4 5 6 7 8 9 10

To the leaders who are dedicated to making their organizations places where people can thrive. Who choose courage over comfort, connection over control, and purpose over performance alone. This book is for you. For your steady presence, thoughtful questions, and belief that better is always worth building. You are shaping cultures where people can flourish. And that deeply matters.

Contents

FOREWORD BY

Ray Dalio

What you and those you work with are like + How you are with each other = **Your Success**

If you know what people are like, you can know what you can expect from them. Understanding them and putting them together well will be the keys to your organization's effectiveness.

I learned this to be true in building my company Bridgewater Associates from being just me and two others in a two-bedroom apartment to over 1,500 people operating as the largest hedge fund in the world. People always asked me what the root cause of our success was - was it the good investment process that we made? Was it something about me and my talent personally? No, the most important cause was what the people and the culture were like. Of course, I, with my partners, shaped it like a head coach shapes a team, but it was what the team was like and the culture that determined how they were with each other that made everything happen.

Culture is a way of being with each other based on shared values. It is built out in a machine that consists of rules, protocols, and tools for people to work with and is essentially what produces your outcomes. It determines how people connect, communicate, and make decisions.

If that machine doesn't work well, the organization won't work well, and even the best strategy in the world will fail.

The challenge for most organizations' leaders is that even though they recognize that culture matters, they don't know what's most important to focus on, how to measure it, and what to do to improve it. They treat it as something intuitive and imprecise rather than as a system, and as a result, they fall short in building great cultures.

It's for this reason that I've been so pleased to collaborate with Jamie Shapiro. A few years ago, I set up a company called Principles to help other organizations drive culture change using the tools and principles I had developed at Bridgewater. Jamie has been a close partner to the Principles team, conducting the rigorous, evidence-based research necessary to gather actionable culture data and deliver real transformation in organizations. The 5Cs model she developed out of that research and shares for the first time here in "Connected Culture" provides not only a clear and practical picture of some of the most important realities teams face - including how to build more openness and transparency, which I believe are essential elements of a successful culture - it also describes the practical levers to pull to optimize performance.

Helping leaders understand those key realities has been the basis of our partnership, and her book is packed with insights and answers to the critical question: How do I get the culture right?

Introduction

If you believe that high-performing teams and a thriving culture are essential to success, you're right. But here's the challenge: After more than 25 years of leading inside organizations and coaching executives (specializing with CEOs), I've seen that most leaders simply don't know how to build both in a way that truly lasts.

I want you to imagine what it would feel like to know that you stepped in at the low point of your company, and through your leadership and role-modeling, you led your team to true high performance, creating a culture that people are proud of. Your legacy shows that people and business outcomes flourish together and that creating a thriving culture is the foundation of business success.

Although this dream is not impossible, it remains the exception rather than the rule. After 15 years of research, McKinsey found that only 30 percent of culture transformations are successful.[1] Unfortunately, high-performing teams represent a minority within organizations, with only 18 percent of senior leadership teams[2] and 30 percent of all teams functioning in this manner.[3]

Team and culture transformation can feel elusive; they are big and take time. People may give up too soon because they don't have a road map, don't understand how the pieces are interconnected, or don't see change fast enough. Improving teams and culture feels intangible until it can be measured. As management consultant Peter Drucker said, "You can't manage what you can't measure."[4]

And that's the inspiration behind the creation of the evidence-based model you'll learn about in this book.

Why Engagement Isn't Enough

Engagement is one of the most commonly used organizational metrics for the health of a company's culture; however, CEOs increasingly recognize that only measuring engagement falls short of creating real cultural transformation. Why is that? Because measuring and getting results about the level of people's engagement is not enough to improve it.

Engagement is defined as the emotional connection and commitment a person has to their job, team, and organization. It's an outcome that all companies strive to achieve because a highly engaged team is more productive, with positive morale and high retention. Sadly, engagement has fallen flat in 2022, 2023, and 2024, remaining below pre-pandemic levels. In the first quarter of 2024, US engagement hit an 11-year low, with a slight improvement in the second quarter of 2024, according to Gallup.[5] The reality is that organizations can't simply measure engagement and expect different results.

I often speak with leaders who are concerned about low engagement scores but don't have a complete understanding on why they go up or down each year. Without this knowledge, they don't have assurance that the engagement initiatives they focus on will make a difference.

The problem is that they haven't measured the key levers that move the needle to improve engagement. To explain this concept, my colleague and partner in the creation of the 5Cs Model, Principles CEO Zack Wieder, shares the metaphor of the "swing versus the shot." If you're a golfer, you know that you won't improve your game by only looking at your score at the end of each round (that is, how many good or bad shots you hit). You improve your game by focusing on the mechanics of your swing and improving your technique. The quality of each shot will vary depending on a number of factors, but the way to make all of your shots better over time is by focusing on your swing.

Organizations struggle to improve engagement because they keep measuring whether they played a good or bad round (as in their annual engagement), rather than focusing on the actual swing (as in the fundamental elements that are driving it and can lead to better outcomes). To transform culture, companies must understand and measure the elements that create highly productive and cohesive teams and thriving cultures. Given this picture, it's no surprise that about 70 percent of culture transformations fail, according to McKinsey.[6] Ultimately, enhancing engagement requires a long-term focus on transforming culture with the right framework and model for measurement.

The Gap

I created the 5Cs Model of Team Cohesion and Thriving Organizational Culture from a need for a road map for both my clients and myself. Despite the growing awareness of the positive correlation between well-being, performance, and healthy work environments over the last couple of decades, I have continuously faced challenges in demonstrating how our work is iterative and interconnected. Team and organizational development is a journey that requires time, tools, and intentionality. Before I developed the 5Cs Model, I often found myself explaining to leaders that every topic and exercise we engaged in during team coaching sessions built upon one another. I tried to illustrate these connections as effectively as possible, but teams often felt disconnected from our journey without a clear framework.

I am primarily a practitioner, but I am also a researcher who is passionate about bringing the business world the most current research and thought leadership from academia. As I looked around for a model for both teams *and* culture, I came up short. Either the models lacked up-to-date research, or they were so complicated that it took too much investment to make them come to life.

For many leaders and organizations, the quest to build high-performing teams and thriving cultures feels like throwing darts haphazardly at a dartboard, hoping that something will hit the bullseye. People often perceive each new initiative as the "flavor of the week" versus a true cohesive strategy. The constant cycle of chasing trends without a solid evidence-based approach leaves people feeling frustrated, lost in the process, and ultimately disengaged. As a CEO, you don't have time to sift through all the research, theories, management books, or academic papers to know what the right approach is.

One of the main reasons it is difficult for leaders is that there is a huge gap spanning years or even decades between when research is conducted and when the research becomes prevalent in the business world. For example, Amy Edmondson, a Harvard Business School professor, coined the term *psychological safety* in 1999 as part of her PhD dissertation research. Her findings showed that psychological safety, feeling safe to speak up without fear of negative consequences, is critical for team success. Her findings were published academically, which is standard practice for scholarly research. However, the term psychological safety would continue to be unfamiliar in the business world until 2016, when *The New York Times* covered a Google project that proved Edmondson's findings. (You'll learn more about that project and psychological safety in Chapter 3.)

You shouldn't have to wait seventeen years (or even one!) to get critical insights on how to optimize your team or organization. And now you don't. The 5Cs Model will equip you with the tools, techniques, and tactics essential for sustainable success. It is an evidence-based model, grounded in current research and built to meet academic standards of validity and reliability (see Appendix for details on the measurement tool) —yet it remains simple, easy to apply, and practical for real-world leadership.

So let's dive in, beginning with a story that may sound familiar if you're a CEO tasked with improving teams and culture.

CHAPTER 1

You Are Not Alone

Lena entered the executive leadership team meeting with her direct reports, prepared to discuss the necessary changes to strategically align the business. On her way to the meeting, she passed the company's core values, which were prominently displayed on the wall, yet none seemed ingrained in her team's behaviors. The team had been deliberating on these changes for several weeks without reaching a final decision. Lena had taken on the CEO role at Covara Global, a publicly traded multi-billion-dollar company, one year ago. Her direct report team consisted of superstars who all possessed a high level of expertise. It had been difficult to understand why they were not functioning as a high-performing team. She had observed a decline in the team engagement scores over the past year, with no clear understanding of the root cause. Given the falling stock price, industry pressures, and shareholder frustration, Lena needed this team to operate at their full capacity. If she couldn't shift the team dynamic soon, Lena knew the board's confidence and perhaps her tenure could be next.

As the meeting began, she kept waiting for the real conversation to start. Everyone was saying half-truths, polished fragments of their perspectives, and not expressing their complete viewpoints. The discussion felt unproductive, circular, and frustrating. Lena knew people weren't fully sharing their perspectives because over the past four weeks, every single person in that room had been in her office at some point to weigh in on what this new structure should look like. She repeatedly pushed to get the team to speak up, share their viewpoint openly, and drive toward a decision. Unfortunately, the conversation stayed on the surface, with no progress made toward a resolution.

Lena was exhausted and unsure how to get this team operating at a different level. She had been trying hard to determine where to focus to get these talented executives to collaborate and stop operating in silos. Over the past year, the company had been diligently working to shift from a fear-based culture, which was focused on order-taking rather than true leadership, to one that was founded on trust, where people felt empowered, valued, and encouraged to lead the business.

At that moment, Lena wondered if, despite her best efforts, fear was still holding her team back. After the meeting, she watched the team break off into selective one-on-one conversations. She knew in her gut that the "meetings after the meeting" had started—the sessions where each executive turned to their most trusted colleagues and actually spoke their mind. Lena felt a sense of dread, not knowing where to start with her team. If she couldn't even get them functioning at the right level, how would she change the company's culture?

Watching her team splinter into hallway huddles instead of standing united made something clear to Lena: They didn't just need alignment—they required transformation. And it had to start with her. She didn't need another reorg or slide deck. She needed a way to build trust, surface truth, and get this team working together like never before. She needed a new kind of road map.

The CEO Weight

Covara Global and Lena are not a real company or CEO, but rather representations of the many clients I have had the opportunity to coach over the years. If you're like Lena, you've recently stepped into the CEO role and worked hard for this moment, with many twists and turns along the way. Perhaps you have walked into a company that doesn't yet reflect your hopes, dreams, or heart. The legacy you want to leave here feels miles away. You know the culture is lacking, fear feels pervasive at every turn, and your team—who you believe are the right people—is nowhere close to a cohesive unit. You feel the pressure from your board, employees, shareholders, and most intensely, yourself. It is a lot to take in all at once, especially when your wiring means failure is not an option.

As you stare down this massive undertaking, the business strategy feels more accessible than the people system, but you know that Peter Drucker's quote "Culture eats strategy for breakfast" is true. So the question in your mind is, where do you start when it feels overwhelming, elusive, and convoluted?

Here is the good news: I've got you. I mean it. I will help you, step-by-step, create the kind of team and organization you've dreamed about. As a public company CEO coach and organizational psychologist, I have had the joy of coaching extraordinary leaders just like you. You are not alone in this journey.

Within these pages, I will introduce you to a framework for creating a cohesive, high-performing team and a culture that people wake up on Monday morning excited to belong to. I have spent my career working with leaders just like you, helping them side by side on the path to becoming the kind of CEO they knew they could be.

Culture Starts at the Top

How you and your team show up daily and interact with one another and the organization as a whole set the tone. As CEO, your behavior becomes culture. What you reinforce, what you tolerate, and how you respond all signal what your team takes as truth. What constitutes organizational culture? The mission, vision, purpose, and core values are often included. These elements are the visible aspects.

There are also invisible elements—such as norms, beliefs, and practices—that are equally important but aren't always given attention. They drive how work gets done. The culture must be experienced day-to-day to be most impactful. This includes rewarding people for demonstrating behaviors that align with it. When individuals aren't living the culture and being rewarded for the associated behaviors, there is a disconnect.

For example, when leaders speak to their teams about the importance of taking time to recharge from work, yet frequently expect them to respond to emails during evenings and weekends, it sends a conflicting message. This can be based on a disconnect between the invisible and visible cultural elements. The leader's message is based on what the culture says it stands for, the visible aspects, yet the leader's actions reveal how the culture actually operates, the invisible aspects.

Defining the core values and behaviors you want to see in your organization is not enough. You and your team must embody them every single day. The spotlight is on you. I know this is a lot to handle, but it is the reality of leading a company. It's why you chose to be a leader: to create an impact that aligns with who you are.

Research consistently shows that the behavior of senior leadership directly impacts organizational performance and culture. Studies from McKinsey indicate that companies with cohesive leadership teams are 1.9 times more likely to outperform competitors[7] and 1.7 times more likely to have higher levels of organizational health.[8] Additional research from Russell Reynolds Associates supports that when CEOs and C-suite teams model desired cultural values and operate cohesively, they set a mirrored standard in the organization, leading to enhanced performance, employee engagement, and overall success.[9]

A report by the Society for Human Resource Management (SHRM) in 2019 found that toxic workplace cultures caused 58 percent of employees to quit their jobs. This turnover cost US employers approximately $223 billion over five years.[10] The SHRM report also highlighted that toxic cultures adversely affect employee well-being, decreasing productivity and increasing absenteeism. Employees in such environments are more likely to experience stress and burnout, further impacting organizational performance.

Eagle Hill Consulting surveyed C-suite leaders and found that 72 percent of executives agreed that corporate culture impacts financial performance. Still, less than half (46 percent) hold themselves and their teams accountable for the culture.[11] This research indicates a disconnect between the importance executives place on team and culture and the investments and actions they make.

I often share with leaders that it is essential to focus on controlling the controllables. The good news is that creating a high-performing, cohesive team and thriving culture is within your control. It is something you can positively impact every single day. It takes intentionality, focus, and care. When executive teams work seamlessly together, modeling effective Collaboration for the organization, it creates a positive ripple effect. Ultimately, the executive teams that function at peak levels deliver superior results and have the workplaces and cultures that people want to be a part of.

In the upcoming chapters, I will give you the road map to make this possible, and I know you will make it happen.

Our Journey Ahead

The 5Cs Model is the result of years of research and hands-on experience, bringing together decades of academic insight and real-world lessons from working with leaders, teams, and organizations. Partnering with expert psychologists and psychometricians, we ran multiple rounds of testing to ensure the model was both scientifically valid and practical to use. What emerged is a framework that hadn't existed before: clear, evidence-based, and grounded in what actually drives thriving teams and organizational cultures. It not only gives leaders a road map, it is also a reliable way to measure progress along the way. In this book, I will explain the framework in detail, showing you how to take each step forward at a pace that makes sense for you, your team, and the organization.

The 5Cs of Team Cohesion and Thriving Organizational Culture

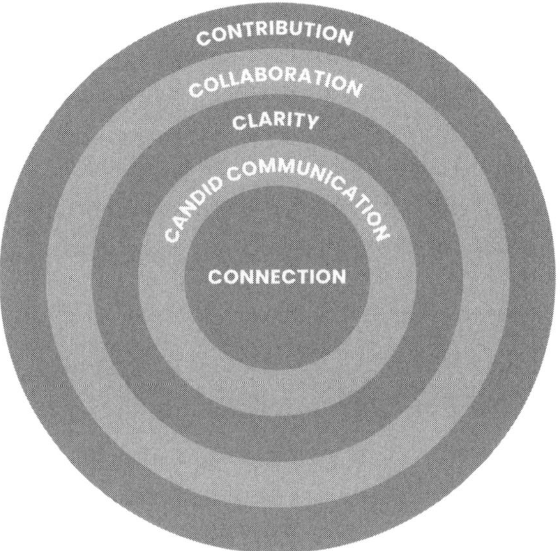

Before we dive into the 5Cs, it's important to know they aren't standalone concepts, they're deeply interconnected. Each one strengthens the others, and together, they create the conditions for teams and organizations to thrive. What follows is a brief overview of each factor, which we'll explore more deeply in the chapters ahead.

Connection within a team and organization reflects the ties that everyone feels with the entity's ethos and with their colleagues. It encapsulates a deep sense of mutual trust that goes beyond mere association or involvement and well-being, including the team and organization members' physical, mental, and emotional health.

Why It's Important: Trust and the sense that people care about each other as human beings are the two key aspects of all high-performing teams. Although it may seem straightforward, these elements enable teams to integrate into every single layer of the model.

Candid Communication is about straightforward, unambiguous discourse among all team and organization members. It can be fostered through psychological safety, which is seen in people's willingness to take interpersonal risks, the two-way processes of healthy conflict and feedback, the transparency and openness of information sharing, and an idea meritocracy that reflects leaders' and managers' willingness to listen to ideas.

Why It's Important: Having a trust foundation is essential for Candid Communication. The more teams are open and honest with each other with care, the better they perform.

Clarity within a team and organization refers to how clear people are about their responsibilities, the processes they follow, and the overarching goals. Clarity can be achieved by delineating roles and responsibilities and their associated expectations, providing well-defined workflows and processes, and creating and constantly striving toward shared goals.

Why It's Important: When teams and organizations understand what they are trying to accomplish together by knowing their roles, goals, and how to achieve them, it minimizes conflict and optimizes efficiency.

Collaboration measures how well people support (and hold each other accountable for) their performance. It is reflected through the existence of strong team support, commitment to accountability in a fair and consistent way, and a drive toward excellence in team and individual performance.

> Why It's Important: Effective Collaboration allows teams and organizations to work together seamlessly, helping each other be the best individually and collectively.

Contribution reflects how team actions align with the organization's core values, goals, and impact. It incorporates the impact that the team and organization have on the broader community, the existence and acceptance of key core values that drive actions and discussions, and the recognition of meaning and mattering. Contributions include the company-wide alignment around a shared vision that provides both direction and purpose.

> Why It's Important: Employees and teams often feel their work isn't meaningful or recognized. One key reason this occurs is that they don't understand how their Contributions align with the bigger picture. When organizations recognize employees effectively and align individual roles with the company's broader values, goals, and impact, the results are increased motivation and performance.

The 5Cs Model provides a holistic view of both organizational and team culture. The five elements are key to fostering a healthy, high-performing team environment and workplace. Our research suggests that they account for roughly half the variance in all employee job satisfaction and nearly 80 percent of the variance in employee satisfaction with the organization's culture. Research from Kotter & Heskett found that companies with high-performance cultures can achieve remarkable financial growth as well. These organizations outpace their industry peers in net income growth by up to 756 percent over 11 years, while those with weak cultures barely grow at around 1 percent.[12] Furthermore, companies with strong, high-trust cultures consistently outperform their industry by factors as high as 3.68 times in stock market returns.[13]

Throughout this book, you will learn how to implement the 5Cs Model and bring it to life within your team and organization. I am honored to be your partner on this journey, and I know this framework will help you leave a legacy that you can be proud of, along with lasting financial success.

CHAPTER 2

Connection

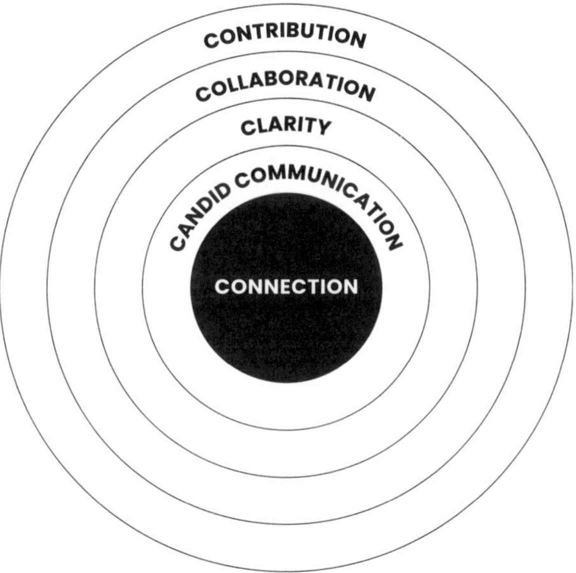

The first time I met Lena, I was struck by her genuineness, kindness, directness, and deep intellect. I immediately felt the strength of her character and leadership. She had a heavy lift in front of her to focus on the organization's future, build her leadership team into a high-performing group, and create the kind of legacy she was deeply proud of. I could see in her eyes that she was frustrated and unsure of where to start. She shared several stories about her leadership team with me, including her constant need to triangulate conflicts; the recent circular,

unproductive meeting; and a feeling like she was on an island at times. With the current team dynamics, Lena felt that everything was a priority, yet nothing was moving in the right direction.

Lena also expressed her desire to optimize the organizational culture. She understood that transformations typically took around three years and felt she lacked a road map to navigate the journey. She shared a recent conversation that she had with her Chief Culture Officer, Dave. Lena and Dave had been searching for something to represent the cultural journey Covara was undertaking. They both wanted to help the organization see the path ahead and identify their initial focus, but they struggled to find something meaningful to ground their efforts. Lena articulated how overwhelming it felt to know there was so much work to do with her team and even more to tackle within the organization.

As a first step, I joined an executive leadership meeting to observe the current dynamic and give Lena some initial feedback. The meeting was pleasant, with everyone sharing the status of major initiatives. At times, I watched people respond to emails or check their phones and not engage in the conversation. After an hour, the only thing that seemed to get accomplished was a high-level overview of the business. Everyone took their turn, but there was almost no real interaction. The other thing I noticed was the propensity to report that everything was on track, on budget, and moving in the right direction, with no risks or concerns being shared. Given the business challenges that Lena had shared with me, I was surprised by this.

For instance, the COO assured the team that fulfillment was running smoothly, even though on-time delivery had declined by nearly 20 percent over the past two months. Inventory levels were misaligned with demand forecasts, and customer complaints were steadily rising, yet none of these issues surfaced in the updates. It was clear there was a reluctance to raise concerns, driven by an underlying fear that doing so would lead to blame and finger-pointing rather than problem-solving. By framing status updates to paint a rosy picture, the COO shielded the team from the truth, delaying critical decisions and hiding the operational issues that needed attention.

After the meeting, Lena and I sat down to debrief. The first question I asked her was, "Does this team care about each other?"

She was visibly surprised and responded, "Why is that your first question?"

I explained that the heart of team performance and thriving cultures starts with two critical questions:

- *Do you care about me?*
- *Can I trust you?*

If you can answer yes to both, then you are moving in the right direction.

Imagine for a moment a relationship in your life where you feel deeply cared for and have complete trust. One where you know that your mental, physical, and emotional well-being matters. Now think about what that relationship unlocks in you and what becomes possible for you in this connected bond.

Were you thinking of someone in your personal life or your professional life?

Chances are, the person who came to mind is not someone you work with, but if it is, then you have an incredible advantage. Working in cohesive, high-performing teams is one of the most powerful experiences a person can have. It allows a person to grow to new levels and accomplish things that are truly outstanding. Additionally, Gallup has shared research that shows that having a best friend at work is the number one predictor of job satisfaction.[14]

Why is that? The fact is that we are human beings. I know, it's so obvious, but we seem to forget in the workplace that our humanity matters. We are people getting exceptional things done together, but we have a misperception that our personal needs must take a back seat. Nothing could be further from the truth. The strength of our relationships in the workplace creates the foundation for team performance and thriving cultures.

That is why Connection is the heart of the 5Cs Model and, through our research, has been shown to be the most critical factor of them all. In fact, Connection has the greatest impact on every other ring of the 5Cs Model.

Connection: The Heart of the 5Cs

Connection reflects the level of bond everyone feels with each other. It encompasses the subfactors of trust and well-being. These two aspects allow teams and organizations to build into every single layer of the model. Connection within a team and organization reflects the ties that everyone feels with the entity's ethos and with their colleagues. It encapsulates a deep sense of mutual trust that goes beyond mere association or involvement, and a well-being that includes the physical, mental, and emotional health of the team and organization members.

Our research results reveal that Connection is the superpower for improving team cohesion and culture. Connection is the most significant ring of the 5Cs and impacts every other ring more significantly than the others. Connection is also the individual element most predictive of job satisfaction, though all 5Cs combined are even more predictive.

Unfortunately, according to Gallup, people's trust in leadership and belief that their organization cares about their well-being hit new lows in 2024.[15] Low-Connection environments don't allow teams and organizations to produce the maximum level of results. People often feel isolated or disconnected from their peers or the organization's culture. Overall, it creates an environment where all other elements of the 5Cs suffer. The subfactors of trust and well-being are intricately linked. Low levels of trust have physiological implications and actually change our brain chemistry. Low trust is linked with being in a state of increased fear, where we feel threatened, act reactively, can't think clearly, and therefore tend to create silos. It's not an environment where people can do their best work or lean on each other.

When well-being is low, individuals don't feel that the team and organization adequately support them. They don't feel cared about as a whole person, that self-care is valued, or that their mental health is supported. Low levels of well-being can impact employees' overall satisfaction and performance. It creates a negative environment, adversely impacting individuals, teams, and the organization.

The wonderful news is that environments of high trust and care create an upward spiral of openness and engagement. To outsiders, it can look like teams are accomplishing the impossible. Magic happens when teams and organizations achieve something much greater than the sum of their parts.

High Connection is the heart of how organizations accomplish all aspects of what they want to achieve. A high-performing team works effectively together, leans on each other, and gets into positive cycles for their own growth. In a high-trust environment, people feel safe, collaborate, and use their full cognitive abilities. In a *Harvard Business Review* (HBR) article "The Neuroscience of Trust," Paul Zak found through his research that "people at high-trust companies report: 74% less stress, 106% more energy at work, 50% higher productivity, 13% fewer sick days, 76% more engagement, 29% more satisfaction with their lives, and 40% less burnout."[16] When well-being is high, everyone demonstrates they care about people mentally, physically, and emotionally, which allows teams and organizations to progress to the next level of performance.

Connection emphasizes bringing greater humanity to the workplace. We must place trust and well-being at the center of how organizations operate and integrate both aspects into how we approach improving leaders, teams, and organizations.

Here is an awesome piece of research: When others see the best in us, we have more access to our best selves. Deci and Ryan, the originators of Self-Determination Theory, highlight that people thrive when their needs for competence, autonomy, and relatedness are met.[17] That sense of relatedness is foundational, feeling seen, valued, and connected.

Now, let's break down the subfactors in more detail and give you the road map to start.

Trust

Trust is one of the most widely researched concepts in team dynamics. While there are many ways to define it, let's start with the most cited definition of team trust in academia: "The willingness of a party to be vulnerable to the actions of another party based on the expectations that the other will perform a particular action important to the trustor, irrespective of the ability to monitor or control that other party."[18]

There is a lot to unpack in that definition. The key to making things stick in our brains is actually to create simplicity. Our brains really only remember three to five things at a time, so my goal is to make things easy to remember. If you remember something, you will share it, and language is foundational to creating culture. I appreciate many definitions and models of trust, but I don't use them in practice due to their complexity.

Building trust and being trustworthy should always be at the top of your mind as a CEO. For these reasons, I gravitate to a modified version of the Trusted Advisor's Trust Equation.[19]

The Trust Equation outlines the core behaviors that foster trustworthiness. It centers on the idea that we have the greatest control over our own actions—both in how we extend trust (willingness to take a risk on someone) and how we demonstrate that we can be trusted (ability to be relied upon). Traditionally, the equation is composed of three elements in the numerator—credibility, reliability, and intimacy—divided by self-orientation. Notably, the model's definition of intimacy aligns closely with Brené Brown's research on vulnerability, which highlights the power of openness and emotional risk-taking in building trust.[20] In light of her work and the broader academic consensus around trust, substituting "intimacy" with "vulnerability" offers a more precise reflection of the behavior that builds trust. This reframing shifts the numerator to this formula:

$$\frac{\text{(Credibility + Reliability + Vulnerability)}}{\text{Self-Orientation}}$$

Here is how each element is defined.

- **Credibility** is a functional expertise and mastery of your craft. While essential, it's often the least significant element in the equation of building trust, since being good at your job doesn't necessarily make you trustworthy. Yet it is what people focus on the most.
- **Reliability** means consistently doing what you say you will do. Being dependable and having actions that can be counted on significantly contribute to trust.
- **Vulnerability:** In her book *Daring Greatly*, Brené Brown defines vulnerability as "uncertainty, risk, and emotional exposure. Vulnerability is sharing with people who have earned the right to hear our stories and our experiences. [It] is not a weakness; it's our most accurate measure of courage."[21] Leaders who express vulnerability by admitting when they don't know something, asking questions, or seeking help model behaviors that foster trust within their teams.
- **Self-Orientation:** Those high in self-orientation tend to be self-obsessed—only caring about themselves and not others—resulting in low levels of trustworthiness. Conversely, those with

> low self-orientation come across as intentionally concerned about the needs of others and have high levels of trustworthiness. It is the difference between an "I" mindset and a "we" mindset. The orientation people have can be self-centered ("me orientation") or team-centered ("we orientation"). A "me orientation" can undermine trust, even if the individual is strong in the numerator aspects. Even with strong credibility, reliability, and vulnerability, a predominant "me orientation" can negate these positive qualities, emphasizing the importance of a "we orientation" in building effective team dynamics.

You are likely to be perceived as trustworthy by displaying credibility when you speak, showing reliability through your actions, demonstrating vulnerability, and lastly, showing your team orientation.

When working with teams, I use this model as an anchor point to discuss the elements of trust. I often find that teams focus much more on credibility and reliability while almost ignoring the importance of vulnerability, and that they lack the awareness to bring the team mindset to the forefront. Thus, much of my work in building trust is focused on the importance of vulnerability and the team mindset.

The research on the importance of trust is extensive, and I could spend this entire book citing the incredible studies that have been done. Instead, I am going to share just a few that highlight the importance of this concept in teams and cultures.

The first study is a meta-analysis: a study of other studies that looks at the body of research on a concept and shares the findings of the research collectively. A meta-analysis in 2023 of the concept of trust analyzed data from 112 independent studies encompassing 7,763 teams and confirmed the importance of trust in team performance.[22] Another study broadly showed that teams with higher levels of trust in their leaders have stronger cohesion and a greater sense of unity, fostering collaboration and alignment toward shared goals. This study also showed that trust enhances people's commitment to the organization, making them more engaged and less likely to leave.[23] Finally, in the book *The Leadership Challenge*, James Kouzes and Barry Posner share that high-trust cultures encourage collaboration, engagement, and a shared sense of purpose. Trust enables open communication and fosters environments where people feel safe.[24]

As I mentioned, trust helps build every other ring of the 5Cs Model. High-trust environments are not only the foundation for team performance and thriving cultures, they also greatly enhance our well-being. Another meta-analysis from 2024 that examined 132 primary studies with a total of more than a million participants showed a strong connection between trust and well-being.[25]

When we are in high-trust environments, we feel safe. We produce high levels of oxytocin, which has been "shown to facilitate collaboration and teamwork."[26] We act responsively, with access to our full cognitive abilities, including clear thinking and problem-solving. Alternatively, when we are in a low-trust environment, we are in a state of fear and cortisol is high. We feel threatened and get into a fight, flight, or freeze mode. We tend to act reactively and don't have access to think clearly. High levels of trust are linked with low fear; low levels of trust lead to high fear. Whether we are in a high- or low-trust situation literally changes not only our interactions but also our brain chemistry.

In human relationships, trust is foundational. Without trust, we cannot forge a strong, connected relationship, and therefore can't have strong, connected teams or cultures.

Taking Action: Trust

There are two keys that create the most powerful unlock when it comes to building trust: listening on a deeper level and sharing your vulnerability. I cannot stress enough how essential it is to truly listen to one another. If there were only one leadership skill and team capability that I could teach, it would be true listening.

Yet as we've seen, it's common for us not to be fully present or to actively listen in conversations, as we often find ourselves distracted, caught up in our own thoughts or formulating a response. This prevents us from truly hearing the other person. Actively listening—being fully present and asking curious questions—provides the opportunity for the other person to feel completely seen and heard, which is incredibly connecting. When you focus your full attention on the person you are communicating with, you listen with curiosity. Being truly present with someone and fully invested in what they are saying allows you to not only hear the words they are speaking but also to tune in to their body language, tone, and emotions. You pay attention to the details of what they are saying instead of just waiting for your turn to respond.

We often believe our primary role and value as leaders is to solve problems. This is not the case. Human beings have a fundamental need to be seen, heard, and acknowledged. Listening creates the opportunity for a person to truly hear another person rather than respond with an answer or a solution. While this might feel simple, there is a reason it's something many people struggle with. Our brain's natural tendency is to react quickly with our own thinking, not fully take in what others are saying and then react. True listening is a two-step process that requires presence, patience, and self-regulation all at the same time. It's not just hearing someone's words; it's quieting your own inner dialogue, resisting the urge to solve, fix, or respond immediately, and instead creating enough psychological space for the other person to feel fully heard.

To become a better, more complete listener, practice asking curious questions and actively listening to the responses. Curious, open-ended questions that start with "how" or "what" encourage deep thinking and personal exploration, whereas closed, information-gathering questions are designed to draw out specific answers. Let go of wanting to hear a yes/no response or solve the problem, and be open to exploring. Through active listening, we can create more trust with each other and, ultimately, with our teams. Not only is listening powerful one-on-one and from a team perspective, but listening to the people within an organization coupled with action is a key to creating thriving cultures.

Take just 60 seconds and try this. Ask someone "How are you doing?" and then do something surprisingly difficult: Say nothing. Just actively listen. No interruptions, no rushing to respond, no relating, no problem-solving. Notice how quickly your mind wants to jump in, offer advice, or steer the conversation. That's the point. This simple act reveals just how much intentional focus real listening requires and how rarely we truly give it.

Covara Builds Trust

The next Covara executive leadership meeting was a team-focused facilitated session. We spent an entire day purely focused on how the team was working together, including establishing new team norms for the meeting, like being fully present and actively listening to one another. There were certainly some skeptics on the team who felt an entire day of team-building was unnecessary, but Lena knew it was an essential step and committed not only to this session but also to regular off-site meetings focused on optimizing the team for the rest of the year.

As a first step, the team took the 5Cs team assessment to establish a baseline and determine where we needed to focus first. (The reason we developed the 5Cs Model as well as the tool to measure it was for this reason. Knowing where to focus first does not need to be a guessing game for a team or organization. You will learn more about the assessment and how to access it in Chapter 7.)

In our meeting, we reviewed the 5Cs Model, shared the science behind the framework, and debriefed the team on their results. It was clear from the data that the team was lacking trust, so that needed to be our primary focus. During the first two hours of our session, the team learned more about each other than they had in a year of working together. For the first time, people shared their leadership journeys and what had brought them to Covara as the rest of the group listened with deep curiosity. The skeptics in the room started to appreciate how the team was evolving through this seemingly simple exercise. The team members began to see the best in one another, creating a deeper sense of relatedness.

Dave, the Chief Culture Officer, also wanted to start building more organizational trust through listening. One of the first things Lena and Dave did in Covara's culture journey was to redefine the company's core values with the expanded leadership team. Dave understood the importance of ensuring that the values reflected the entire company, not just the leadership perspective. To facilitate the broader organization's views, Dave enabled others throughout the company to listen deeply to each other. He created a framework for listening sessions to take place at every level of the company, gathering perspectives and, ultimately, a deep understanding of what the core values should be. After over 200 listening sessions, led completely by volunteers within the company, there was enough qualitative data to identify five core values for Covara.

While core values are a wonderful compass and anchor point for culture, they are meaningless if they just become words on the wall without behaviors backing them up. Core values only become real when they're embedded in daily behavior; they must be observable in action and noticeably absent when not displayed. Living core values often requires people to stretch beyond their comfort zones, because the behaviors they call for are rarely simple or automatic. It's like staying fit. Operating in ways that enhance our effectiveness demands intention, courage, and a daily commitment, even when it's hard.

Based on the extensive feedback from the organization, Covara took the time to thoughtfully define its key behaviors, enabling its core values to come to life daily. Another key to building trust in teams and organizations is the power of vulnerability. Being vulnerable takes courage. As Brené Brown shares in her book *Daring Greatly*, "Vulnerability is the first thing I look for in you and the last thing I'm willing to show you in me."[27] The Covara leadership team experienced the positive impact of vulnerability firsthand during their session when they opened up and shared their authentic selves with one another.

As a leader, you are responsible for modeling ideal behavior to foster a culture of trust. If you, as a leader, aren't willing to show up with vulnerability, then you can't expect others to do so.

I want to be thoughtful about how I talk about vulnerability, as the concept can be overemphasized at times. None of us has permission to be 100 percent vulnerable all the time in the workplace. It is not beneficial to always speak your mind. Being vulnerable at work doesn't mean sharing every thought, emotion, or detail of your personal life. It means being willing to ask for help, lean on others, admit mistakes, and recognize strengths and growth opportunities. It is important to discern where and with whom it is appropriate to express yourself fully, including sharing both positive and negative emotions. When what really matters goes unspoken, it's worth asking: Is this a culture where people can truly thrive?

Vulnerability is also expressed through authenticity. Specifically, this means being true to your moral compass, integrity, principles, and core values. Another way to practice vulnerability is to share your own well-being journey, which gives others permission to do the same.

Well-Being

Well-being is continually overlooked as a key to team performance and thriving cultures. My specialization as a researcher has focused on clarifying these connections. Well-being in the 5Cs focuses on the team and organization's emphasis on physical, mental, and emotional health. It essentially answers the question: Do you care about me as a human being, beyond just my output or performance?

Well-being is not a perk. It's not a yoga class or a fruit bowl in the kitchen. Too often, organizations equate wellness with programming—standalone efforts that may be well-intentioned but remain disconnected from how the organization actually operates. True well-being is culture-deep. It's embedded into daily interactions, into meeting norms, into how leaders show up. It's seen when leaders model boundaries, encourage recovery, and design systems that support, not deplete, energy. That's the difference.

The most effective teams I've worked with don't treat well-being as something extra, they recognize it as essential. They don't ask, "How do we do more with less?" They ask, "How do we design work in a way that sustains performance over time?" The fact that this is not emphasized blows my mind. It is the core of our needs as people. Leaders who focus on caring for their teams and also care for themselves are able to create the highest levels of performance.

My research focus has been on leadership vitality. Vitality is defined as positive aliveness; it is the inner resource that includes physical, psychological, emotional, and spiritual energy. It is on the opposite end of the spectrum from burnout. Prioritizing well-being isn't about lowering performance or not working hard; it's about understanding how we work in ways that sustain energy, finding the right rhythms of rest and replenishment for ourselves and our teams. Through my research, I have been able to show that the building blocks of well-being create the needed vitality for leaders to reach their full capacity.

In one study, I interviewed two dozen Fortune 1000 CEOs to understand their perceptions of vitality within their daily life. The aim was to learn more about two opposing ends of the spectrum: vitality versus burnout. It focused on addressing these two questions:

What does leadership performance look like when we are highly vital?

What does it look like when we are drained?

The results revealed that leaders who possess vitality can transfer their energy to their teams, foster positive and inclusive environments, engage with others, uplift those around them, and maintain the enthusiasm and mental agility to excel in their roles.[28] Conversely, when leaders are depleted, they create negative environments for those around them by being closed off, showing less gratitude, and appearing more irritable, discouraged, or disengaged.

My research highlights that vitality is key to how we show up every day. A foundation of vitality gives leaders the abundance of energy needed for themselves, to share with others, and to meet the demands of their worlds. Yet vitality is an underfocused piece of the puzzle of leadership, teams, and organizations.[29]

Research shows that well-being at work is declining, with headlines including these from 2024.

"Workforce well-being continues to stall."[30]

"People's mental well-being has been worsening."[31]

Given the collective challenges we're facing and the redefinition of work from the COVID-19 pandemic, the results are not surprising. However, the research only gives a partial view. Workforce well-being—driven mostly by corporate wellness programs or one-off initiatives—has had the same focus for far too long, with lower results in recent years. These programs don't encompass what it truly means to flourish in the workplace, and it's likely we'll continue to see deterioration unless we do something different. Making a real improvement requires fully integrating well-being into the business and day-to-day operations as a foundation for leadership, team, and organizational culture. Systemic change needs to happen to truly improve workforce well-being.

Our mindsets surrounding work and well-being need recalibration. In corporate America, we still operate with "busy badges," meaning the belief that we must be busy every second of the day to be most productive. While that is absolutely inaccurate, it is still a prevalent view—despite the fact that research shows leaders perform at their best when maximizing their well-being (including creating space in their days). To be successful means fundamentally changing how each part of the corporate system operates to include well-being, recognizing how it is central to team performance and organizational culture. Fostering a commitment to caring for people is essential to unlocking an organization's full potential.

Taking Action: Well-Being

For well-being to become integrated within the organization, it must start with leaders changing their mindsets, recognizing that well-being is foundational to leadership, team, and organizational performance. By building your vitality, you can access your full leadership capacity. When you foster your well-being, you show up at your best and positively impact others. You have a lot of energy going out into the world. What about energy coming in? You must learn how to cultivate your energy to meet the incessant demands you face.

Prioritizing your well-being is how you get your main source of energy. You can start by building awareness of your own energy resources, including what fills and drains your energy and how to refuel. This is an individual experience. It is up to you to determine what energizes you every day. The first step of growth is awareness. Own your well-being, and prioritize it so it becomes the norm and not the exception. Remove the "busy badge" and recognize that it negatively impacts your teams and organization when you lead with it. For instance, take a leader who publicly champions well-being but consistently schedules back-to-back meetings from early morning through late evening, rarely takes time off, and celebrates team members who "power through" exhaustion. Even without saying a word, this behavior sets a tone that endurance is valued more than restoration, and that visibility matters more than sustainability. Over time, this creates a culture where burnout is normalized and well-being becomes performative rather than real.

Next, recalibrate your mindset about what it means to lead with foundations of well-being. A healthy team culture starts with the leader modeling the behaviors that promote well-being. Create the space in team meetings and off-sites to build strong relationships where you demonstrate that you value the whole person, care about your team members' energy resources, and ensure they aren't depleted in the workplace.

Covara Prioritizes Well-Being

When I first started working with the leadership team at Covara, it was clear that their well-being had taken a back seat. People were working around the clock, weekends included. One look at their calendars showed back-to-back meetings with no time to think, transition from one task to another, or even care for their basic needs. They had a team culture of "firefighting," creating less long-term strategic thinking and no time for reflection or growth from lessons learned. Well-being was seen as a luxury not afforded to top executives, which led to colds running rampant on the team.

To address this, we had to do two things: bring awareness to the issue and shift the team culture. Covara started with simple agreements, for example that working on the weekend was reserved for urgent issues only. The team also agreed to open up the conversation with one another about well-being and be more candid about their energy or lack thereof. While these may seem overly simple, they were the first steps in the journey back to integrating well-being into their leadership.

Meeting Culture

Another place where you can take immediate action is creating a meeting culture that fosters both trust and care. There is a lot I could say about creating more efficient and productive meetings, but I am going to focus for now on how to cultivate more Connection. I will address the other topics when we get to Clarity in Chapter 4.

Meeting culture is a commonly overlooked opportunity to advance organizational and team dynamics. Yet where do we spend the majority of our work time? In meetings. So take care to prioritize Connection at the beginning of each meeting—and not just through a simple icebreaker question. While this can be fun at times, asking about someone's favorite ice cream flavor doesn't often lead to the results you are hoping for. Instead, consider starting the meeting with a meaningful question that acknowledges and shows care for the whole person. This will create an opportunity for people to connect on a deeper level, which will develop trust.

Here are some examples.

- How is everyone feeling, on a scale of 1 to 10?
- How is your energy: green, yellow, or red?
- What area do you need the team's help on?

By making that an agreement and focus at the start of the meeting, you can also create an environment with increased active listening.

You can also incorporate more well-being into your meetings by recognizing that people are not meant to sit all day without opportunities to move, eat, or drink. Incorporate movement and opportunities for them to refuel their bodies during or between meetings.

Here are some additional strategies:

- Get creative about the meeting environment: Go outside, hold meetings in different places, have standing or walking meetings, or put chairs in a circle with no table.
- Encourage eating and drinking during meetings.
- Give time for breaks between meetings so everyone can care for their physical bodies. For instance, change meeting durations across your entire team and/or organization from one hour to 45 minutes or from 30 minutes to 20 minutes. This will support people by giving them thinking space and transition time.
- Have a no-meeting "lunch hour" so everyone can refuel with food and move their bodies on a daily basis.

The heart of the 5Cs Model is creating a healthy organizational and team culture, with foundations in trust and well-being. This allows every other factor to reach its full capacity. Focusing on improving Connection will positively impact all other elements of the 5Cs: Candid Communication, Clarity, Collaboration, and Contribution.

Ultimately, the Connection element emphasizes bringing greater humanity into the workplace. We must place trust and well-being at the center of how organizations operate and integrate both aspects into how we approach improving leaders, teams, and organizations. When teams feel truly connected—grounded in trust and well-being—they create conditions where honest, candid conversations can finally take root. And that's where we head next.

Key Takeaways

Connection embodies mutual trust that transcends simple association or involvement and encompasses the physical, mental, and emotional well-being of both the team and organization members.
Trust can be broken down into credibility, reliability, vulnerability, and minimizing self-orientation.
Encourage active listening to build more trust.
Leaders who focus on caring for their teams and also care for themselves are able to create the highest levels of performance.
A simple and immediate way to integrate well-being into the workplace is to shift meeting culture by starting meetings with a meaningful question that acknowledges and shows care for the whole person.

Main Barriers to Overcome

Undervaluing trust and well-being: Too often, Connection is seen as a "nice to have" rather than a performance driver. Without a foundation of trust and genuine care, Connection remains surface-level and is not optimized. Leaders must learn to prioritize both, not just as cultural goals but as business imperatives.

Superficial relationships: We struggle with vulnerability, the very thing that makes Connection possible. This paradox sits at the heart of why Connection is hard: We crave realness in others but often fear the risk of revealing it ourselves. For leaders, embracing vulnerability means going first, sharing what's real, owning missteps, and showing your team that strength includes uncertainty, not the absence of it.

CHAPTER 3

Candid Communication

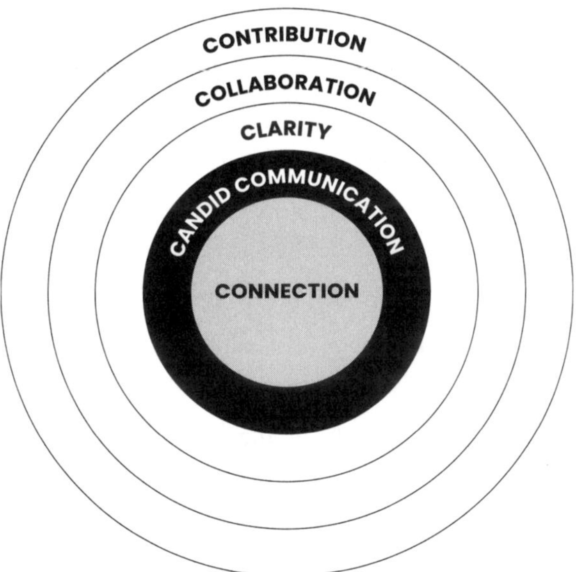

As the Covara Leadership Team began to build a solid foundation in Connection, we moved to expand their capacity for Candid Communication. It was clear from their behavior with each other that they needed more courage and practice in this area. As a first step, we conducted a Live Team 360. This is a simple but powerful exercise where each team member shares one behavior the team is consistently doing

that has the greatest impact on its performance and one that, if the team did more of, would improve the team's effectiveness. The team did a great job expressing some of the behavioral strengths, including taking the time to check in with each other more one-on-one, being more open about where they needed help and the space they were taking between meetings and in meetings. When it came to discussing growth opportunities, the first few comments were overly safe and surface-level.

Finally, Lena's Chief of Staff Andy went deeper. He expressed that when he shared his perspective, it was often not acknowledged by the team, which made him feel less valued. This wasn't just feedback—it was vulnerability in action. Andy was taking a risk; he feared that by speaking up, he would damage the relationships he cared so much about, but he knew things needed to change. You could see the genuine surprise from the rest of the team. I knew that this was such a pivotal moment: How the team responded would shape the rest of the conversation.

Giving feedback requires even more courage than receiving it. And the way someone responds determines whether they'll be trusted with feedback again.

Lena responded first to Andy, saying, "Thank you so much for being open about how you feel, Andy. Your courage to take this conversation to a deeper level serves as a role model for us all."

Andy took a deep breath and sat back a little. Lena continued by expressing her ownership of his experience and how she would approach things differently in the future.

Lena is often the first person in the room willing to say "I don't know. I messed up. I am learning, and I want people to push back on my thinking." She gives everyone around her permission to strive for excellence instead of perfection. She rejects the conventional and outdated paradigms of what a CEO is supposed to look and sound like in favor of a more human heart-connected and authentic version of this role. When people meet Lena, they are immediately struck by her down-to-earth communication style. Her authenticity doesn't just create Connection—it also creates safety. There is no doubt in my mind that Andy spoke up in this meeting because of the safe space Lena had created.

The rest of the team followed Lena's lead and talked through how they could all be more aware in their interactions with Andy. The remaining Live Team 360 was real, transparent, and productive. The team committed to giving each other more positive and constructive feedback in the future, which meant they would need to lean in to discomfort, resist the urge to stay silent, and choose honesty even when it felt risky. The Live Team 360 ended up being a big step forward in the team's Candid Communication.

As the title of this factor suggests, Candid Communication is about open, straightforward, unambiguous dialogue within a team and organization. It's about cultivating an environment where people are transparent, direct, and free from hidden agendas. It is about the ability to be truly open in our communication. Candid Communication means telling the truth—with care. It's the practice of speaking openly, directly, and respectfully, even when it's uncomfortable. It requires courage and emotional maturity. This openness facilitates information flow, leading to an atmosphere where the foundation of trust gets further extended.

Our research found that Candid Communication is the best performance predictor of all the factors.

The tension in Candid Communication lies in our desire to be honest while also wanting to be liked, avoid conflict, or protect relationships. We fear saying the wrong thing or creating discomfort, so *we soften, delay, or avoid the conversation altogether. At the heart of this challenge is a deeper conflict: the pull between our short-term and long-term selves. In the short term, it feels easier to sidestep hard truths. But in doing so, we sacrifice the long-term outcomes we care about like honesty, alignment, and mutual respect. Leadership is about recognizing and managing this tension. It takes courage to choose short-term discomfort in service of long-term goals. And the paradox is this: The very disconnection we fear is often what Candid Communication helps prevent. When candor is absent, issues go underground. Decisions get made without full context. Innovation stalls. And people begin to disengage—not because they don't care, but because they no longer believe their voice matters.*

Candid Communication is built through the strong core of Connection. Without both, you don't get the best from people. In your role as a leader, getting people to say what they honestly think around you is one of the hardest and most crucial things you can do. CEOs often don't get the truth for several reasons that will be detailed in this chapter. Cultivating an environment around you where people share their ideas, their issues, and themselves is key to achieving true performance.

Courage and Candid Communication

Candid Communication is the factor a majority of people find the most difficult. It takes courage backed by vulnerability to speak what you need to say.

My favorite definition of courage is "Courage is not the absence of fear; rather it is being afraid and taking action anyway."

Why is it so hard just to speak honestly and create an environment where others can do the same?

My role as a coach is both incredibly simple and complex. It is simple because at the core of us as human beings, we have foundational needs like love, belonging, and the desire to be seen, heard, and acknowledged. Yet the complexity comes from the many layers, masks, and stories we put on top of those basic needs. As a coach, often my work is to seek out the most foundational need and try to meet it.

Imagine if we had permission from one another to communicate at our most basic levels. It would create a foundation of Connection that fosters creativity, innovation, transparency, constructive feedback loops, healthy conflict, and exceptional levels of growth. Candid Communication doesn't always go smoothly. We might say too much or not enough, or express ourselves in a way that doesn't land well. And the truth is, we will mess up. But when there's real Connection with trust and care, we can return to each other, revisit the conversation, and make it right. It's not always comfortable, but it's how we learn and grow. The goal isn't to be perfect. It's to be open enough to keep trying, keep listening, and keep getting better together. It takes courage to keep showing up with honesty, especially when it would be easier to stay silent.

One of the reasons Lena instills courage in others like Andy is because of her authentic leadership style. In a 2011 study that explored the relationship between authentic leadership and courage, findings highlighted the critical role of a leader's authentic leadership on instilling courage in others even in times of adversity.[32] Courage gives us access to speak candidly with others. The HBR article entitled "Why Employees Are Afraid to Speak" outlines key barriers that prevent people from speaking up in the workplace, highlighting fear of negative consequences as a primary deterrent.[33] This underscores the importance of fostering a culture of courage for open communication.

Additionally, the concept of workplace courage is examined in the article by Jim Detert and Evan Bruno titled "The Courage to Be Candid," which identified 35 behaviors viewed as courageous by employees, many of which involve honest communication, such as challenging superiors or giving constructive feedback to peers.[34] The findings suggest that these courageous behaviors when done well promote personal, team, and organizational growth, emphasizing the pivotal role of courage in facilitating open and honest dialogue.

Finally, several studies by HBR professor and author Amy Edmondson show that high levels of Candid Communication correlate with increased morale and engagement, driving better organizational outcomes.[35] And as I mentioned previously, our research also found that Candid Communication is the strongest predictor of performance across all the factors we studied.

How do we foster a courageous environment that enhances Candid Communication? Through focusing on its critical subfactors:

- Psychological safety
- Healthy conflict and feedback
- Transparency
- Idea meritocracy

Let's look at each one in more detail so you can understand them better.

Psychological Safety

Psychological safety refers to the degree to which employees feel secure in expressing concerns, vulnerabilities, and dissenting views without fear of retaliation. As I mentioned in the introduction, Edmondson coined the term "psychological safety" in 1999 as part of her PhD dissertation research. She was studying the healthcare sector, specifically hospital systems and nursing teams, to identify what makes a high-performing team. When she reviewed her data, she noticed that the high-performing teams had more errors recorded in the system. Edmondson didn't understand what was happening. Whenever researchers encounter a large amount of data that doesn't make sense, they keep digging and try to uncover what can be learned from it. She soon realized that the high-performing nursing teams weren't making more errors; they were just reporting them, which allowed them to address and fix those errors. In contrast, the non-high-performing teams weren't reporting the errors and also were not fixing them.

Edmondson discovered that it wasn't just individual willingness but also the team environment that allowed people to speak up about errors. That enabling condition was what she defined as psychological safety, and it was critical to team success. Although her findings were published academically, the term *psychological safety* would continue to be an unfamiliar concept in the business world for years. It took Project Aristotle, a study conducted in 2012 at Google, for psychological safety to become prevalent in the workplace. This project set out to research what factors led to the highest-performing team in a two-year study spanning 180 teams. The results showed that psychological safety was the most critical factor in team effectiveness, confirming Edmondson's research findings.[36]

People are often confused about the difference between trust and psychological safety, and these terms are often used interchangeably. The main distinction is that trust is between two people, while psychological safety describes a group's climate or culture. Teams and cultures that have a lot of trust lead to psychologically safe environments. Vulnerability is our greatest access point to building both.

Interestingly, when we hypothesized the subfactors of the 5Cs, we initially included psychological safety in the Connection ring. However, through research and testing, we learned that it was actually a subfactor of Candid Communication. This makes sense when you dive into the definition and see that psychological safety is demonstrated through a willingness for people to say what they honestly think.

When I first started sharing the importance of this subfactor, many organizations pushed back, saying it was not something they thought people would be willing to embrace, that it was too academic of a concept, and that prioritizing psychological safety would undermine accountability. Psychological safety is often misunderstood as being about keeping everyone comfortable, feeling good, or being nice. This misunderstanding is actually a sign that psychological safety might be absent. Psychological safety is about creating a culture where people can challenge each other, speak hard truths, and engage in productive tension without fear of judgment or retaliation.

We must also separate the continuums of psychological safety and accountability. They are different and, ultimately, we aim to build both. Having high standards, ownership, and accountability are essential for organizations, and combining this with psychological safety creates the highest-performing teams and organizations. As for the term being too academic, I have continually shared the data and importance of this concept to help organizations embrace it.

One of my favorite quotes that I heard David Cooperrider say is

> "What you focus on grows, and what you think about expands."

This quote succinctly describes our brains. We experience something called *selective attention*, which determines how we perceive the world around us. With so much information bombarding our brains simultaneously, we can't absorb everything all at once; thus, our brains process only what we choose to focus on. We focus selectively based on the lens we look through.[37]

This also brings in the psychological concept of *inattentional blindness*, which is when we fail to notice a fully visible but unexpected object, event, or stimulus because our attention is engaged elsewhere.[38]

I always teach these two concepts when discussing psychological safety. The reason is that without awareness of psychological safety and the mechanisms to build it, people frequently overlook opportunities. Selective attention and inattentional blindness also apply more broadly in the conversation about teams and culture; without a focus on these areas, people often miss the ways to build it. The 5Cs is a road map to create a lens for culture to bring more awareness and ability to act.

When people have psychological safety, they show up more authentically, feel comfortable admitting mistakes, learn from failure, and share new ideas. This ultimately leads to better decisions and more innovation. As Ray Dalio shares in his book *Principles*, "Create an environment where it's okay to make mistakes, but unacceptable not to learn from them."[39] Unfortunately, when we have the opposite, we have cultures of fear, where people are afraid of messing up, tend to blame others, and hold back helpful perspectives and ideas. Decision-making suffers. We also can't create cultures of belonging when we don't have psychological safety.

Psychological safety fosters many benefits in organizations, including calculated risk-taking, empowerment to speak openly, more creativity, quicker innovation, increased ability to adapt to change, and the unlocking of the benefits of diversity. People know they can stick their necks out without getting their heads cut off. This unlocks a new gear for the organization to operate in.

A meta-analytical review of psychological safety conducted in 2017 looked at 136 independent samples encompassing over 22,000 individuals and nearly 5,000 groups. They found that the outcomes of high psychological safety include increased task performance, higher team performance, and increased levels of people going above and beyond their job responsibilities.[40]

Taking Action: Psychological Safety

One of the questions I get repeatedly is how a leader creates an environment of psychological safety. The answer from Edmondson lies in focusing on three attributes of leadership: humility, curiosity, and empathy.[41]

- **Humility** gives you greater access to vulnerability, understanding that you don't always have to have the answer. Instead, you can say you need help, and lean on those around you.

- **Curiosity** taps into the essential active listening discussed in the previous chapter.
- **Empathy** helps you access the feelings of others to create necessary space.

If you own those three areas of your leadership every day, you will naturally cultivate psychological safety. Openly communicate the significance of psychological safety and its benefits for performance, creativity, and engagement. Most importantly, though, your words and actions must match. Psychological safety is built through consistency in action, even when it's hard. Leaders must make a daily choice to create an environment of psychological safety through their actions, their words, and the behaviors they model in every interaction. If a leader sets a clear expectation around performance or behavior and then follows through by holding others accountable when that expectation isn't met, it strengthens the psychological safety. Why? Because people see that words and actions are aligned. Leaders need to model the behaviors they wish to see throughout the organization. This includes showing vulnerability, admitting mistakes, and responding to feedback constructively.

If you talk about the importance of psychological safety but then behave in ways that contradict it, you will degrade everything you said. For example, if someone comes to you with constructive feedback, which takes an incredible amount of courage and vulnerability, and you react poorly, that is the quickest way to ensure you will never receive feedback from that person again. If you want to build teams and a culture with psychological safety, you must ensure that your words and actions are congruent.

You can also consider your role in meetings. Make sure you are listening first and asking questions like these:

- What is a different perspective or point of view?
- What am I missing?
- What should we be learning?

You often hear people say that leaders should speak last in meetings. I will share a different perspective: Leaders need to set the tone up front for conversations to feel safe. This can be done by sharing things like "I want to hear different perspectives, and it is my intention to make this an open, comfortable conversation," or taking the time at the start of a meeting to create the agreements needed to get the most out of the discussion. These are all tools to promote more psychological safety in the room. Then spend time listening and asking questions during the conversation, and if you have a strong opinion, share it. Don't leave people guessing what you are thinking. The more open you are, the more open others will be. If the conversation veers into conflict, help guide the discussion back in a healthy direction.

Healthy Conflict and Feedback

The Healthy Conflict and Feedback subfactor of Candid Communication focuses on having a culture that encourages a diversity of perspectives and the giving and receiving of clear and constructive feedback across the organization. When healthy conflict is absent, we often see toxic positivity, where everything is reported positively and on track—even when things are actually breaking. We also see people agreeing in meetings but then complaining afterward to the person they feel closest to.

Another sign is the waiting-out behavior that occurs when people won't speak up but instead think that if they just wait out the leadership without taking real action, the issue will go away. People often mistake a healthy conflict issue with a commitment issue. I have heard time and time again that the perception is that people are unwilling to take ownership or commit to the direction, when in reality the issue is that healthy conflict is absent. Study after study confirms the importance of diverse perspectives in making solid decisions, fostering creativity, and driving innovation. Significant research shows that diverse teams make better business decisions up to 87 percent of the time compared to individual decision-makers.[42]

One issue that tends to arise is that people don't have clarity around the difference between task and relationship conflict. *Task conflict* is disagreement around the work itself, like the tasks, goals, processes, or strategies. *Relationship conflict* is rooted in personal issues, emotions, or interpersonal difficulties between people. When people confuse these two, it leads to further disconnection.

For example, imagine two teammates disagree on an approach to a project. This is an example of a task conflict, but one person perceives it as a personal attack on their intelligence. In reality, the task is something the two people should be able to openly discuss from their different perspectives, but instead, it turns into something completely different.

Think about this: Where do you confuse the two in your life? As a CEO, you've likely found yourself in situations where a board member's idea isn't fully aligned with the company's direction, but challenging them might feel like a threat to the relationship, so you say nothing. Or perhaps you've held back from addressing a misstep on your team—not because the issue wasn't important, but because you worried it might create personal tension or make you seem overly critical. These are examples of the common confusion between task and relationship conflict. We avoid necessary conversations about the work, fearing they'll be taken personally. But healthy organizations depend on leaders who can distinguish between the two and who create space for open debate, challenge ideas with respect, and address issues directly.

Teams and organizations that have healthy task conflicts have enhanced team performance by encouraging critical evaluation and diverse perspectives. However, the research also shows that when task and relationship conflict are intertwined, the opposite is true.[43] It's essential to cultivate teams and cultures that are rich in healthy task conflict while at the same time have strategies to address relationship conflict productively. As Adam Grant highlights in his book *Think Again*, the absence of conflict isn't harmony—it's apathy. He emphasizes that healthy conflict, particularly task conflict, is essential for innovation and growth.[44]

It is not surprising that environments with a foundation of psychological safety make task conflict more productive and lead to higher performance. Our brains are wired in a way that makes conflict hard. First, we tend to see conflict as a threat sending us into flight, fight, freeze, and fawn responses and out of our deep level of thinking. We are also oriented to seek agreement as a first step and tend to focus on convincing others to see our point of view. Both responses can lead to highly unproductive conversations.

The first step in healthy conflict is to accept that we all have different perspectives, styles, and comfort levels in these conversations.

Be aware of your own orientation and be respectful of that of others. Embrace the idea that a diversity of perspectives will ultimately lead you to the best outcomes. Start with this mindset for healthy task conflict.

The next step is to leverage the physical body to calm the mind. Deep breathing allows you to get out of your reactivity and back into the prefrontal cortex, where profound thinking can happen.

Next, find alignment and purpose in the conversation. This is such a critical step yet so often missed. You can look at this as the stake in the ground, the thing that you need to come back to repeatedly in the conversation. For example, if you are having a healthy conflict conversation about having a more engaged team, you may have different perspectives on how to accomplish this, but the stake in the ground is that you both want higher engagement on the team.

A more personal example for me was around parenting our son Jack. My husband and I had different perspectives on how to get him to focus on his homework when he was younger. Where we started the conversation, though, was with the stake in the ground about our common goal of wanting to instill in him the core value of hard work. The conversation became so much easier once we had our alignment and purpose for the discussion.

Alignment usually creates positive emotions in people, which according to emotions expert Barbara Fredrickson, broadens and builds our thoughts, connection, and willingness to take action.[45] Instead of starting in a place of reactivity, we can start the conflict in a place of Connection.

It's no surprise that the next step is listening. Listening is truly the number one skill in leadership. When you actively listen during any conversation, especially a conflict discussion, you give people the space to have their perspectives heard and acknowledged. Studies on conflict resolution emphasize that when individuals feel their perspectives are acknowledged, they are more open to engaging in future interactions and collaborations, even amidst disagreements, and are more willing to commit to ideas and directions, even if they initially disagree.[46]

The final step is agreement. After people have shared their perspectives and actively listened to one another, the goal is to find the place of agreement to move forward. As Ray Dalio writes in his work on thoughtful disagreement, the goal isn't to avoid conflict but to engage in it with curiosity and respect, because doing so leads not only to more effective decision-making but also to stronger relationships.[47]

When it comes to relationship conflict, the good news is that you can apply the same steps in the conversation to move through it productively. Accept the fact that you are coming into the conversation with different viewpoints and comfort levels, find the stake in the ground together (like acknowledging that this relationship matters to you both), listen actively, and find a place to move forward together.

The biggest distinction in handling these is that task conflict is typically addressed as a team, while relationship conflict is best managed one-on-one or with only those directly involved. Above all, a foundation of care and respect is essential in all healthy conflict situations. One of the most beneficial actions teams can take to reduce relationship conflict is to raise awareness of the varying personality preferences within the group. Understanding our differences in thinking, engagement, and motivation can help individuals learn more about themselves and one another. (I will expand on this further in Chapter 5: Collaboration.)

One area of healthy conflict that is often missed but is also essential for cohesiveness is constructive feedback. I have learned a great amount about this from the brilliant founder of Shift Positive, Pete Berridge.[48] I want to share some of the essential principles that can transform how people, teams, and organizations create cultures of constructive feedback.

First, most people are not taught effective ways to give and receive feedback. Many concepts like *radical candor* have been taken to an extreme and often lead to even further degradation of constructive feedback. People give feedback in ways that are not founded in care and then use the excuse that they were just being radically candid. No, you were just being an asshole. Constructive feedback is founded in care and thoughtfulness, and it is solution-oriented. When people experience feedback that lacks care, they often swing in the opposite direction and stay silent to avoid hurting people's feelings. This is not the answer either because withholding feedback deprives others of the clarity they need to grow. The answer is in learning how to give truly constructive feedback.

Most feedback is problem-focused without specific behavioral descriptions that help the receiver understand the information. People send feedback over the fence without taking the time to think through the behavioral solutions that would be effective for the change. For example, telling someone that they are talking too much in a meeting can lead to someone being withdrawn and disengaged, when the real hope was for the person to listen more actively and ask more curious questions.

The receiver of feedback may try to adjust but never truly know whether they are hitting the mark. The unspecific, problem-focused feedback can trigger a defensive response and ultimately leave the receiver feeling deflated, confused, and unable to grow. In 2019, Gallup reported that only 26 percent of people strongly agreed that the feedback they received helped to improve their performance.[49]

To create healthy cycles of constructive feedback, you need to focus on two key things: solutions orientation and support. Emphasizing solutions versus problems helps people receive feedback more easily and understand the specific behaviors they need to change. It shifts the focus to actions that are needed more versus less. Regarding selective attention and inattentional blindness, when the feedback giver knows what they are looking for from the other person, they will see it and be able to positively reinforce it. This creates positive cycles of reinforcement, which are more effective for behavioral change than negative reinforcement.

Feedback should also be an active, two-way commitment. Once the giver shares their feedback, they should be an active participant in the person's growth, creating support.

One of the best questions I ever received about constructive feedback was "What is the difference between feedback and judgment?" My answer was "Care." When we create cycles of constructive feedback founded in care and support, we enable the best opportunities for growth.

Taking Action: Healthy Conflict and Feedback

The first action step with healthy conflict is to ask yourself the question: How comfortable do I feel in a conflict?

We all have different preferences, and it is foundational to know whether conflict is far outside your comfort zone. If it is a stretch, that just means it will take more energy, not that you aren't good at it.

There are two additional tools that make a big difference when stepping into conflict. The first is the power of assuming positive intent. A favorite quote of mine by Wayne Dyer speaks to this.

> "When you change the way you look at things, the things you look at change![50]"

Assuming positive intent can transform how you see a situation or another person. When you look through the lens of positivity, you may see new angles and perspectives.

In the field of psychology, we make a distinction between *realistic optimism* and *delusional optimism*.[51] Realistic optimism is about taking information that can be interpreted in multiple ways and putting a positive lens on it. In contrast, delusional optimism is taking an overly positive mindset and ignoring contrary evidence and facts. You should aim for realistic optimism when assuming positive intent. If assuming positive intent is not possible in a situation, the next best thing is to lean in to curiosity.

Another critical step in healthy conflict is separating facts or data points from story. This is a challenging step. We have something called a *reflexive loop* in our brain.[52] It is the part that takes in information and layers on our assumptions, experiences, and beliefs to create our interpretation. We are story-making machines, and often the narratives we create from the data points are not 100 percent correct. Taking the time to separate the facts from the story in any situation, especially in conflict, can make a big difference in approaching the conversation.

When you are ready to step into the healthy conflict conversation, I encourage you to use the acceptance and alignment steps described in the previous section, actively listen, and find your place of agreement as the last step.

These steps also apply when giving someone constructive feedback. Remember the importance of first aligning around care for the other person and your desire to help them grow. You can literally tell the person why you are giving them feedback. For example, "I want to give you this feedback to help you land your point more clearly in meetings." It is also essential to focus on behavioral solutions rather than the problem. One powerful question to ask before offering feedback is: What are your feedback preferences? We all have them, but people rarely ask until they have something to share. Inquiring about someone's preference for feedback can provide valuable insight for when you actually have something to share.

Another place to emphasize when giving feedback is their strengths. We often focus on constructive feedback, but taking the time to give positive feedback is equally, if not more, important. We tend to stay in our comfort zones as people, which means that at times, we can overuse our strengths to the point that they become opportunities. For example, when overused, a leader's strength in decisiveness can become impatience. Or a strength in empathy can, when unbalanced, lead to difficulty setting boundaries. Feedback becomes more holistic, empowering, and actionable by intentionally highlighting what a person does well and how it might sometimes tip into overuse. This approach helps individuals grow not by abandoning their core strengths, but by learning to calibrate and expand them thoughtfully.

Finally, feedback should be timely. The sooner you can give someone feedback on a situation, the better. Too often, people wait to share feedback until the perfect moment, which never seems to come—or worse, they wait until someone's review. This makes it difficult for the person receiving the feedback to even remember the situation.

Giving feedback isn't easy; it requires vulnerability, yet it is critical for creating cohesive relationships. Remember that when you are giving *or* receiving feedback. The way you respond to someone who's taking the time, energy, and courage to share your growth opportunities determines whether you get that opportunity again. Creating a culture of constructive feedback depends on how you receive feedback when someone is brave enough to give it to you.

Transparency

Transparency within a team and organization relates to the openness and accessibility of information and decision-making processes to all people. A lack of it is one of the biggest complaints I hear across organizations. Think about how many times you have heard that leadership is not being transparent. Sometimes it can feel that even when you go out of your way to share information, people still give you that feedback.

Here is something you should always do as a leader: Communicate, communicate, communicate. Then, when you think you are on the verge of being annoying, communicate more.

Leaders are rarely criticized for overcommunicating, only for undercommunicating. The reality is that you have to say things repeatedly for people to internalize them. I understand that for most high-level leadership roles, full transparency would be unreasonable given the need for confidentiality. Instead, focus on communicating as openly and clearly as your role allows. Research from Deloitte found that transparency in teams and organizations improves performance, job satisfaction, safety, career development, innovation, and organizational agility.[53]

One of the key cultural pillars of Ray Dalio's organization Bridgewater is radical transparency. In his book *Principles*, Ray shares how this approach ensures that essential information and issues are visible rather than concealed, promoting accountability and continuous improvement.[54] His commitment to openness, honesty, and uncovering and addressing the truth in all aspects of work was and continues to be a cornerstone of the Bridgewater culture. Transparency is a foundation for trust and growth because it enables individuals to make sense of things themselves without feeling like they are being spun.

Transparency not only includes access to information; it also reflects our communication style. For example, do we communicate openly with honest, straightforward language, and share only the facts? Or do we tend to be guarded, share our interpretations of facts, and use corporate speak? Using real language instead of the highly complex corporate jargon that often pervades our organizations builds trust and commitment.

For example, there is a significant difference between sharing a difficult moment in the business that requires job cuts and explaining why . . . versus hiding behind complex statements that mask the reality such as "We are strategizing next-generation infrastructures to build for the future." A 2023 multilevel study examined the influence of authentic leadership and relational transparency on team dynamics and performance. The research involved 60 teams, composed of 60 leaders and 245 team members, and found that relational transparency, as a component of authentic leadership, helped cultivate team performance and commitment.[55]

Taking Action: Transparency

The first step in transparency is taking the time to define what that means to you, your team, and your organization. What does open, regular communication look like? Committing to speak openly whenever possible and overcommunicating are two other actions you can take. Here are some more examples.

- Hold regular open meetings where leaders share key information about the organization's performance, challenges, and strategy.
- Take time to explain the rationale behind major decisions.
- Schedule frequent all-hands meetings and regular department meetings to facilitate the flow of information across different levels of the organization.

Also, consider the technology that is enabling transparency within your team and organization. With the ever-increasing access to data and systems, it is essential to think about how information flows through your organization and the access that your people have to it. How can you leverage the systems you already have to increase transparency and access to information? For example, utilizing collaboration tools for real-time information sharing, creating central repositories for documents and information, and facilitating access to business data and analytics. The most important action you can take, though, is being a role model for transparency in every interaction and decision-making process.

Idea Meritocracy

Idea meritocracy refers to the willingness of others, especially leaders and managers, to listen to ideas based on their merit, regardless of where they come from. It is essential for building high-performing teams and thriving organizational cultures, as it prioritizes the quality of ideas over roles, positions, or status in an organization. When organizations create environments where individuals feel safe to express their ideas openly, they drive better decisions and outcomes. This approach encourages the open dialogue of ideas and allows for the emergence of optimal solutions, regardless of their source.

Edward Hess, author and professor at the University of Florida, has studied examples of companies that have created idea meritocracies, including Google, Intuit, Pixar Animation Studios, and Bridgewater Associates. In those organizations, an idea meritocracy has played a key role in driving consistently high performance and empowering people to share their ideas, challenge the status quo, and explore more with curiosity.[56]

According to Ray Dalio, a healthy idea meritocracy rests on three essential behaviors, which are also critical to the other subfactors of Candid Communication.

- The courage to share honest thoughts
- The skill to engage in thoughtful disagreement

- The discipline to follow agreed-upon processes for resolving differences[57]

As a culture and practice, an idea meritocracy can lead to the highest levels of learning, thinking, listening, and flourishing. In most organizations and industries, the best ideas for innovation come from people who are closest to the customer, but the ideas that get implemented often come from those with the loudest voice or the most authority. Without an idea meritocracy, it is difficult to get ideas that originate close to on-the-ground problems to the top of the organization. Cultivating idea meritocracy gives everyone more voice and empowerment to share their great ideas.

Taking Action: Idea Meritocracy

The good news is that the actions you take around both psychological safety and transparency are keys to creating a culture of idea meritocracy. It is essential to have various channels where people throughout the organization can easily share their ideas, such as a dedicated email address, feedback forms, collaboration platforms, leadership listening tours, and team innovation sessions. These channels give people at all levels the opportunity to share their ideas without barriers and, assuming you have cultivated a culture of psychological safety, without fear of judgment. Giving people both real-time and asynchronous options for sharing ideas allows everyone, regardless of role or schedule, to contribute meaningfully to the organization.

When we prioritize the best ideas over the loudest or most powerful voices, we empower people to help us grow to new levels of innovation and performance.

Think for a moment about what it would be like to know that the best ideas were continually surfaced . . . that people in your organization were dedicated to creating psychologically safe environments . . . that diverse perspectives were regularly sought . . . that there was a commitment to helping one another grow with care . . . and that communication occurred frequently and openly. With a strong core of Connection, this vision can become a reality, but it requires focus and intentionality to implement the Candid Communication ring effectively. Fostering an environment where people share their ideas, concerns, and authentic selves is key to achieving excellent performance.

Covara Embraces Candid Communication

Lena's focus on building a high-performing team and thriving culture at Covara has been a top priority since she stepped into her role. She has been focused, intentional, and transparent, believing that these qualities are essential to her success. Lena has been unwavering in her commitment and her communication. Even in the most challenging times, she makes space to focus on her team's dynamics because she knows the *how* is as powerful as the *what*. She has put culture at the top of her priorities list and understands that thriving cultures take time and focus. At every company meeting, Lena shares the importance of culture to achieving Covara's mission. But most importantly, she models every day the behaviors that she wants the organization around her to adopt. Her Candid Communication and request for the same from others inspire people to open up, share, and communicate in ways that allow Covara to reach its full potential.

Candid Communication isn't easy, but it's essential. It's not about being blunt—it's about being brave. And the best leaders model that bravery, one conversation at a time.

Key Takeaways

Candid Communication is built on the strong core of Connection. Without both, we don't get the best from people.
To build psychological safety, increase humility, curiosity, and empathy.
For healthy conflict and feedback, encourage a diversity of perspectives and be willing to give and receive constructive feedback. Remember, the way you receive feedback can determine whether you will receive it again.
To increase transparency—communicate, communicate, communicate. Then, when you think you are on the verge of being annoying, communicate more.
Prioritize the quality of ideas over role, position, or status in an organization to enhance idea meritocracy.

Main Barriers to Overcome

Avoiding the truth: Many leaders and team members hold back from being candid because they don't want to create tension or hurt someone's feelings. However, avoiding the conversation to protect the relationship often does more harm than good, eroding trust, alignment, and performance over time. Candid Communication takes courage: the courage to speak with honesty, even when it feels hard, and the belief that truth serves the relationship rather than threatening it.

Sounding critical: Without practice or examples to follow, candor can come off as criticism. In this case, we lack the skill and often the modeling to have honest conversations. Candid Communication isn't just about saying what you think; it's about saying it in a way that's clear, respectful, and rooted in care. Leaders must model what it looks like to be both honest and thoughtful at the same time.

CHAPTER 4

Clarity

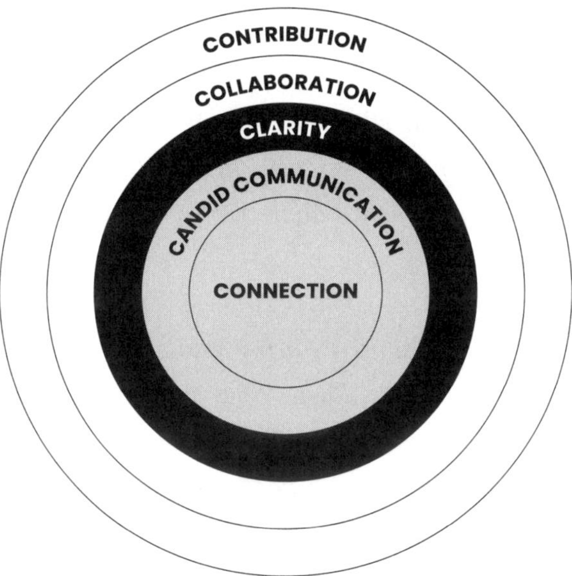

Covara is a matrixed environment, typical of most global and large-scale organizations. Teams span multiple countries and time zones, creating a complex organizational structure that demands a focus on Clarity, particularly during times of change. In environments like these, lack of Clarity doesn't just slow things down—it also breeds frustration, misalignment, and underperformance. CEOs must lead the charge in making Clarity a nonnegotiable part of the organization's operations.

Lena recognized that to maximize shareholder value, there needed to be a more strategic and enterprise-wide focus on marketing as a growth engine for the company. Covara's brand and marketing strategy was primarily decentralized, with each division having dedicated marketing resources. So Lena hired a new Chief Marketing and Growth Officer to set a new direction for Covara. When the new CMO Rachel joined Covara, she was eager to establish a more strategic path for the company's marketing, brand, and growth strategy.

As a first step, Rachel implemented sweeping organizational changes, restructuring the reporting lines so that all marketing resources across the company reported directly to her. This change established a new centralized marketing function. Although this was directionally correct, the lack of Clarity in the implementation created confusion and frustration throughout the company.

Change without Clarity is chaos. And when people don't know who's doing what or how decisions are being made, they default to self-protection, slowing everything down. Roles and responsibilities became unclear between the divisions and headquarters, division presidents struggled to navigate the newly undefined processes for their marketing needs, and goals and priorities were blurred across the company. Duplicative work was happening all throughout the organization, and employees became increasingly territorial and siloed, which was the opposite of what this change intended to achieve. Rachel and Lena were frustrated that such a crucial strategic effort was going nowhere fast. It was time to pause, realign, and assist the leadership team and the organization to get the Clarity needed to make this change a success.

Clarity refers to how clear people are regarding their responsibilities, the processes they follow, and their overarching goals. A high level of Clarity helps to eliminate ambiguities, ensuring that each task and decision is well-informed and purpose-driven. It creates flow. And in high-stakes environments, Clarity allows teams to move fast without breaking trust. However, it seems to get overlooked again and again when it comes to high-performing teams and cultures. Too often, we assume it is obvious—until it's not. The signs are subtle at first: duplicated work, missed deadlines, misaligned priorities. But over time, the cost compounds.

While this factor seems obvious, it is often not an area of focus. Think about how many times you have heard complaints like these:

"My role is unclear."

"I'm not sure who can make that decision."

"I don't know how to get this through the system."

"My priorities are unclear."

When you create more Clarity, you give your team members more comfort in getting their work done effectively. In complex, large systems, this can be a game-changer. If you want to see how fundamental this is, put up a new org chart and watch what happens to the people in the room. They immediately want to know how this impacts them, their role, and their work. Clarity is essential to how individuals, teams, and organizations perform at their best.

Clarity as a Force Multiplier

Clarity is not meant to eliminate flexibility; it's meant for us to understand how we effectively get work done in a complex system. When things are unclear, you often see issues around duplicative work, creating unnecessary conflict and causing people to feel like their time is wasted. They can also feel like others are stepping on their toes and can become overprotective of their work. Clarity is essential, but it doesn't mean overengineering every message or process. When we confuse Clarity with control, we risk creating complexity that stifles momentum instead of fueling it.

As CEO, it's your job to define what great looks like—across roles, workflows, and outcomes. Clarity isn't micromanagement; it's leadership. Your team can't hit a target they can't see, and ambiguity is one of the fastest ways to erode trust, stall momentum, and create rework.

The ideal in teams is that we are in the sandbox together, leaning in and helping one another where possible. While Connection and Candid Communication certainly help make this possible, Clarity tells us how we get work done, what we're responsible for, and what we should focus on. Research shows that establishing clear roles and responsibilities, processes, and goals increases motivation, boosts job satisfaction, and improves performance outcomes, reducing feelings of overwhelm.[58]

Clarity at the broader organizational level is also essential. For example, every large-scale organization like Covara must continually navigate the line between centralization and localization. This concept is called many different things depending on the industry and the company: corporate versus division or region, local versus central, headquarters versus the business. Organizations with more Clarity can adapt more easily to this changing line. As McKinsey & Company highlighted, role and goal Clarity is essential for organizational agility.[59] The shifting line between centralization and localization is just one example of where we need to be able to adapt quickly. Organizations are regularly faced with new information that requires a strategy pivot, a new opportunity to jump on, or an issue that needs immediate focus. With Clarity comes the ability to respond more swiftly to the ever-changing business landscape.

One concern we hear is that too much Clarity causes unnecessary bureaucracy in organizations and makes them unable to adapt to change. In fact, it's quite the opposite: Clarity allows organizations to react faster. Our brains are not wired for uncertainty, so if everything around you is unclear, any additional change or uncertainty will be met with resistance. Clarity gives people more certainty in their day-to-day lives, and therefore, more comfort. With that comes a greater ability to accept ambiguity in times of change and the confidence necessary to venture outside of their comfort zone.

Think for a moment about a time when everything felt unclear. Perhaps you were still figuring out your role, or there were so many priorities on your plate you were unsure about how to even get work moving in some areas. Feeling a little overwhelmed by all this yet? Now, imagine that the board asks you to take on an entirely new project. How do you think you would feel at that moment?

Let's imagine the opposite: You are clear on your goals, priorities, role, and how to get work done effectively. The board asks you to take on this new project. My guess is that you would welcome the opportunity.

This is happening every day throughout your organization. With Clarity, you'll see increased confidence, job satisfaction, well-being, and the ability to adapt to change and performance at the individual, team, and organizational levels.

Roles and Responsibilities

Roles and responsibilities refer to the Clarity and definition of individual tasks, duties, and decisions. When Clarity is high, team members understand their responsibilities—reducing confusion, redundant work, and friction. Role Clarity has been shown to help employees develop positive work attitudes and innovative behavior and to enhance team performance.[60] When people lack Clarity about their roles and responsibilities, it leads to frustration, inefficiencies, and a lack of ownership. This ambiguity can stifle decision-making and reduce overall organizational agility.

We often see this breakdown from the first moment a role is defined within an organization. Creating clear and well-thought-through job descriptions is a great first step in role Clarity. Roles and responsibilities aren't the same as defining tasks; they're the ongoing commitments we own, not just the individual actions we take.

When roles and teams are already in place, it is essential to understand how the team is structured, including the roles within it. People need to understand how to operate effectively within the system. For example, in many teams, single decision-makers are assigned based on the task or project at hand. It doesn't mean that others don't work with the decision-maker; it just means that a single person is accountable for the final decision. While this is often the case, it is not always clearly identified and articulated.

Taking the time to define something as simple as this can go a long way. Having clear and well-documented roles and responsibilities within a team also allows for overlapping work to be more productive, enabling people to understand how and where they can optimize collaboration. In complex systems, roles and responsibilities are not always black and white—there is a lot of gray space. However, when you define where things *are* clear-cut, you give people greater access to play in the gray space.

At an organizational level, Clarity in roles and responsibilities is key to leverage your company's size and scale. Far too often, we see duplicative work across various departments. How many times have you heard that a project is being started or worked on, only to find out months later that it was completed in another department without anyone knowing? Think about data analytics, for example. It's common to see new reports created in different departments conveying the same information. Establishing organizational Clarity in roles and responsibilities creates a greater ability for cross-functional teams to collaborate and leverage their work together.

Taking Action: Roles and Responsibilities

The tool most often used to clarify roles and responsibilities is a RACI matrix, which defines who is **r**esponsible, **a**ccountable, **c**onsulted, and **i**nformed for each task or project.[61]

- **Responsible:** The individual(s) who do(es) the work to complete the task or deliverable
- **Accountable:** The person who ultimately owns the task or decision
- **Consulted:** Those who provide input, expertise, or advice related to the task
- **Informed:** Individuals or groups who need to be kept in the loop about progress or outcomes

This simple and effective framework is a great starting point for clarifying roles and responsibilities in projects, teams, or processes. However, documenting it is just the first step; people also need to internalize what it says, which is often the hardest part. This requires continual practice and learning.

Example: Covara's RACI Matrix in Action

Task/Decision	CMO	Marketing Director	Product Manager	Sales	Finance	IT
Define project strategy	A	R	C	C	C	I
Develop marketing campaign	I	A	R	C	I	I
Finalize product design	I	I	A	C	C	I
Set pricing strategy	I	C	C	C	A	I
Launch sales training	I	C	C	A	I	I
Oversee IT and e-commerce setup	I	C	C	C	C	A
Execute product launch event	I	A	R	C	C	C
Monitor performance & adjust	A	R	C	C	C	I

Rachel decided that a RACI matrix was a crucial first step in helping the marketing and division leadership teams gain Clarity about the new organizational structure. However, even after everything had been documented and shared, teams were still struggling. We decided to do an activity that would help the team understand where the breakdowns were occurring. To help these teams internalize the RACI framework, we conducted an experiential activity that effectively translated the concepts from paper to practice, making the learning experience highly impactful.

Here's how we did it. We had a spacious open room for this activity and a defined RACI chart, which had been filled out for several months. From memory, we asked the team to "act out" the RACI chart. We called out a task for the team and asked the participants to take the following actions:

The accountable leaders were sent to the center of the room.

The responsible leaders were told to circle around the accountable leaders.

The consulted leaders were directed to put a hand on the shoulder of one of the accountable leaders.

The informed leaders were told to fill in around the room.

With each task we called out, we watched the room struggle to move and realize that they still had not internalized the RACI they had defined. This exercise created an opportunity for them to internalize the model even faster.

Using a model or framework like the RACI matrix can illuminate areas of overlap, confusion, and ambiguity. While it takes time up front, it saves an incredible amount of time in the long run. There are several other models for roles and responsibilities, like the RAPID decision-making model (recommend, agree, perform, input, and decide) developed by Bain & Company, which clarifies decision-making roles within organizations. Identifying one that suits your company can serve as a true catalyst for Clarity.

Another tool that can help with roles and responsibilities is having templates for defining new and existing roles. Creating job descriptions that detail specific tasks, responsibilities, and expectations for performance and accountability can give people the Clarity they need.

Here's a great quote attributed to John C. Maxwell to remind you of the necessity of taking action to describe roles and responsibilities

> "Disappointment is the gap between expectations and reality."

Setting expectations for a role can make all the difference in someone's mindset and performance. Finally, use your existing technology platforms to share and communicate the information you define. Clarity can only be leveraged if it is communicated effectively.

Processes

Processes refer to the documentation of operational workflows and systems used by teams and the organization. Process Clarity is not about rigidity or bureaucracy but about creating a scalable foundation and enabling agility. It is a road map for how to get work done effectively, creating task repeatability and ensuring you are not continually reinventing the wheel.

When processes are clear, teams can execute tasks confidently, efficiently, and consistently. Research by Hu and Liden highlighted that process Clarity leads to higher levels of team performance and a greater willingness to go above and beyond for the organization.[62] People who understand how to navigate their work feel more empowered and less stressed, and have greater ownership. They can focus on their work rather than the mechanics of how to accomplish it. When processes are unclear, frustration ensues, deadlines can easily be missed, and people may feel demotivated from having to concentrate more on how to get things moving rather than the actual task at hand.

At the organizational level, process Clarity across departments and divisions is essential. For example, a clear understanding of an end-to-end process across the organization allows for a deeper insight into how the customer is ultimately served. Too often, people do not see the full picture of how their work impacts the customer. A team or division may think their job is complete when, in reality, the handoff or next step is the catalyst to getting the customer served.

When you help create Clarity across an organization, it translates to a deeper understanding of how workflows impact the customer experience. A clearly defined and followed process also gives the customer a consistent experience, which is essential.

Taking Action: Processes

Process isn't everyone's strength, so my recommendation is to identify who the experts are in your organization and lean on them. I'm fortunate to have someone on my team who handles all the operations for our organization who lives and breathes process, which is quite different from me.

Here are a few questions you can ask yourself and others to get started in taking action.

- What processes on our team would be helpful to document or clarify?
- Which processes seem confusing or undefined?
- In which areas could more or less structure create greater efficiency?

It is also essential to connect process to your purpose. When organizations don't, it can feel like the process has no reason other than creating one for the sake of doing so, which can be frustrating for the end user.

One area in which I have experience and can offer insight is the importance of meeting culture and Clarity in helping teams and organizations perform at a higher level. Creating better and clearer processes for meetings can go a long way. Just think about your own schedule for a moment. How many hours do you spend in meetings each week? Now ask yourself: How often do I know the actual purpose of the meeting, receive an agenda or materials in advance, or feel confident that the right people are in the room? If you're like most people, your honest answer is probably "almost never." And that's exactly the problem.

There are basic processes you can implement to make meetings more effective. One very foundational rule is that every meeting invite needs a purpose statement in the description. For example: Is this a brainstorming meeting, a working session, a decision point, or a status update? If it's a status update, question whether that should be a meeting at all. Simply providing the meeting's purpose can help participants understand their roles and who else might need to be included.

Another easy process is to close meetings with action items and assignments, including who is responsible for each task. Meetings often end with ambiguity regarding the next steps, but if you take five minutes to summarize, it could go a long way. It is draining to participate in meetings that feel disorganized and unproductive. By providing the meeting intention and outcomes in advance, the meeting is more productive, giving attendees the ability to participate with greater Clarity and contribute more effectively.

Shared Goals

Shared goals refer to aligning and clarifying team and organizational priorities, objectives, and the resources allocated to achieve them. When teams have shared goals, are aligned around them, and are clear on the results they are striving for, it becomes easier to prioritize and complete work. Teams can collaborate with more motivation and direction.

Goal setting is a topic of ongoing research in organizational psychology. Early concepts like Locke and Latham's goal setting theory explain that creating specific, measurable, and challenging goals unlocks higher performance.[63] Having shared goals that are rewarded collectively also fosters a team mindset.

Effective prioritization is also key to accomplishing shared goals, ensuring that time and resources are allocated to what matters most. It's not enough to have goals; teams must understand how to prioritize their work. When prioritization is unclear, teams struggle to determine what to tackle first and can easily become overwhelmed. Most people have more on their plates than they can accomplish in a day, week, or year. Instead of saying no to new things, we just keep saying yes, yes, yes. This can lead to cycles of being overwhelmed or stuck in firefighting mode, where all we focus on is the most urgent issues that lead to short-term results.

Effective prioritization provides guardrails that keep teams on track, allowing people to adapt more easily to new requests and changes. In fast-paced, ever-changing business environments, knowing which tasks to focus on and when to provide that focus is essential. Shared goals at the organizational level create greater cross-functional alignment and collaboration, helping to prevent the formation of silos. It encourages behaviors that focus on the broader organization and helps people recognize that you are one large team. Organizations and teams with clear goals and priorities are more productive, experience less burnout, and accomplish their work in a more organized way.

Taking Action: Shared Goals

There are several frameworks that can help teams and organizations set goals effectively, such as OKRs (objectives and key results), SMART (specific, measurable, achievable, relevant, time-bound) goals, and measurement frameworks like KPIs (key performance indicators). These highly utilized frameworks can be leveraged for setting and prioritization.

When considering prioritization, one of the tools that stands the test of time is Stephen Covey's Big Rocks philosophy. Leadership will always involve a struggle between our short-term and long-term selves. Covey has a great video from the 1990s that beautifully illustrates this concept. In it, he invites an executive on stage and gives her a bucket half filled with pebbles. He then asks her to make room in the bucket for her big rocks, which are labeled things like major projects, relationships, family, and strategic planning. She struggles to fit the big rocks into the bucket. Next, he provides her with an empty bucket and says, "Let's start over. How can you design your life differently?" She quickly understands that the big rocks must go in the bucket first, allowing the small pebbles to be poured around them. Everything then fits.[64]

This metaphor will always apply. When people, teams, and organizations define their Big Rocks and create the needed space for them first, everything else can fall into place more easily. The issue is that we get caught in cycles of short-term thinking and acting, leading to perpetual cycles of firefighting. Organizations then end up with cultures that reward and enable the hero mentality versus true high-performing teams. This creates more siloed cultures, limited short-term thinking, and difficulty in scaling.

One of the quickest ways to build Clarity is to visualize how time is actually spent. Tools like color-coded calendars reveal misalignments between what matters most and what gets attention. The Eisenhower Matrix is a four-quadrant tool for prioritization. This tool asks individuals or teams to bucket their work into four different quadrants, with the x-axis labeled as "Urgent" and the y-axis as "Important."

The four quadrants end up as follows.[65]

	Urgent	Not Urgent
Important	Reduce	Schedule
Not Important	Delegate	Declutter

- **Quadrant 1: Urgent and Important**
  Recommended action > REDUCE This quadrant includes tasks that demand immediate attention due to their urgency and high impact, such as crises or pressing issues. Reduce time spent in this quadrant by doing more work in Quadrant 2.
- **Quadrant 2: Not Urgent but Important**
  Recommended action > SCHEDULE This quadrant involves future planning through strategic thinking. It requires initiative, with more time being spent here.

- **Quadrant 3: Urgent but Not Important**
  Recommended action > DELEGATE If possible, tasks in this quadrant should be assigned to other team members to promote empowerment and enhance decision-making.
- **Quadrant 4: Not Urgent and Not Important**
  Recommended action > DECLUTTER Eliminate tasks that do not align with the mission and shared goals. Learn to say no to these tasks.

This graph can help clarify the perceived priorities of the individual or team, further aligning people, teams, and the organization overall with the right mindset, workflows, and outcomes.

Clarity is often overlooked in models of team performance and organizational culture. This is a big miss. When you ask people in organizations about their greatest pain points, you will typically hear about one of the subfactors related to this issue. Clarity is what enables work to be completed more seamlessly in complex systems. By focusing on this factor, organizations can help people feel more energized, teams become more productive, and organizations achieve greater alignment. With the core elements of Connection, Candid Communication, and Clarity, the true power of Collaboration can be realized.

Covara Gets Clear on Priorities

Rachel decided that another key to the success of the new marketing organization was creating ease around processes and defining shared goals that spanned both her new organization and the divisions. She convened the leadership teams again to first clarify their shared goals and reprioritize their work as a team. As they engaged in

Candid Communication, Rachel facilitated a dynamic working session where each leader mapped out their priorities and identified areas of overlap or misalignment. Tensions surfaced at times, but with a renewed focus on Clarity, the group found common ground. By the end of the session, they had crafted a unified road map—one that balanced division-specific needs with broader organizational goals. Energized by the Clarity and alignment, the teams left with a shared commitment: to streamline processes, break down silos, and work as a cohesive force to drive Covara's marketing strategy forward.

When roles, goals, and processes are clear, teams gain velocity. But they still need to move together. That's where Collaboration comes in.

Key Takeaways

Clarity doesn't eliminate flexibility—it enables it. When people understand the structure, they can operate with more agility, not less. Improve Clarity of roles and responsibilities through defining individual tasks, assignments, and decisions. When people know what they're responsible for, it reduces confusion, redundant work, and friction.
Process Clarity isn't about rigidity or bureaucracy. It's about building a scalable foundation that enhances agility by clearly defining and documenting operational workflows and systems.
Establishing better and clearer processes for meetings can be a great first step.
When teams have shared goals, align around them, and understand the results they are striving for, it becomes easier to prioritize and complete work. Consider using a framework like Stephen Covey's Big Rocks to help define these shared goals.

Main Barriers to Overcome

Avoidance: We often avoid creating Clarity because we fear it will feel like bureaucracy or overengineering. But Clarity isn't about adding red tape. It's about removing friction. When roles, goals, and processes are clear, people can move faster, make better decisions, and spend less time second-guessing or cleaning up confusion.

Misguided assumptions: We assume Clarity exists when it doesn't and then fail to maintain it over time when it does. Without clearly defined roles, shared goals, and processes, teams often operate on unspoken assumptions that eventually lead to missteps, confusion, or rework. Even when Clarity is created, it's rarely revisited. In fast-paced environments, speed often wins over structure—roles shift, goals evolve, and no one pauses to realign. The result is quiet drift and growing frustration. The solution is to build in regular moments to realign and get Clarity.

CHAPTER 5

Collaboration

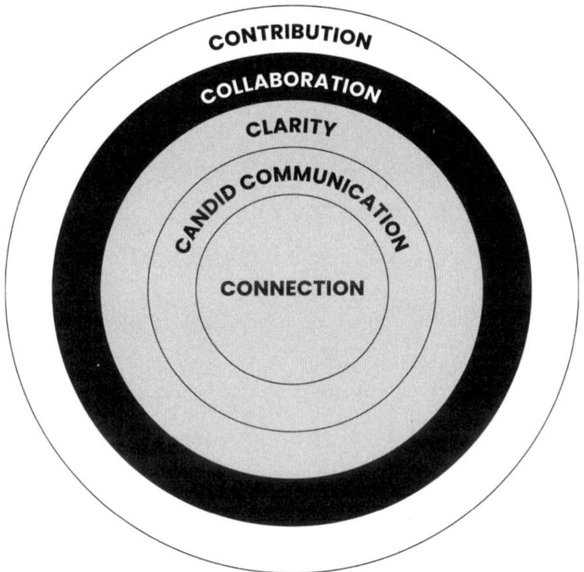

About a year and a half into Covara's cultural transformation, the company hit a monumental business challenge that couldn't be solved by a single leader or team. When the executive leadership became aware of the large-scale issues facing the business, they immediately jumped into action. This is, of course, what any leadership team would do when facing a crisis. However, how they did this is essential to highlight.

The executive leadership team had been focused on their team culture for almost two years at that point. There was a strong foundation of Connection, Candid Communication, and Clarity. The team knew that to solve this crisis, company-wide Collaboration would need to happen immediately.

A large cross-functional leadership team that represented all aspects of the business was pulled together. Now, I will not tell you that things were awesome from the start. In fact, it was quite the opposite.

Another of my favorite Wayne Dyer quotes is "When you squeeze an orange, you get orange juice because that's what's inside."[66] *Character doesn't change under pressure; it's exposed.*

This was a critical moment for Covara's leadership to determine who they really were as a team and culture.

Even with extreme business pressure, could they live the values and behaviors that were the cornerstone of their journey?

Could they form a cross-functional project team that leveraged and leaned in to a culture with Connection, Candid Communication, Clarity, and Collaboration?

The start of the journey felt uncertain, with some big missteps in how the team showed up. But life and business are not about perfection, because there is no such thing in humanity. What this team did, though, is continually strive for excellence together and focus on learning from their missteps and building on their success. Early in the project, the leadership team came together and asked the hard questions of themselves and each other.

Where are we living our culture?

Where are things breaking down?

Each leader was open, honest, and willing to look at themselves in the mirror. They gave each other support and, more importantly, let that support in. I watched as this team adjusted to lead their culture in a way that enabled Collaboration at its highest levels and solved the business issues at lightning speed. The cross-functional project structure became the model for how their business continues to be run today, with a focus on Collaboration across the company.

Collaboration often feels like the crown jewel of teams: an ability to work together and accomplish things, with the equation that one plus one is greater than two. The word collaboration has its roots in the Latin verb collaborare, which is the combination of the prefix "col" (together) and "laborare" (work). It's what sets humans apart in our unparalleled ability to unite and achieve more together than we ever could alone.

In the 5Cs Model, Collaboration refers to how people work together, support one another, strive for excellence, and hold each other accountable for their performance. In a collaborative environment, knowledge is harnessed by encouraging members to learn and grow, helping them exceed the results they could achieve in isolation. When teams and organizations have mastered Collaboration, it feels like anything is possible. To the outside world, it looks like things are being accomplished at record speeds with an ease that is unexplainable. For those on the team, it feels like accomplishing with people who want each other to win together, striving for excellence in a truly supportive environment, and lifting each other up at every opportunity. It is an environment where people work hard and find joy together in the process. It is what I coach on and strive to be a part of always.

Collaboration: The Journey from Colleagues to Teammates

Sometimes the words *teamwork* and *collaboration* are used synonymously, but teamwork is a broader umbrella concept that applies to all the 5Cs. Collaboration, on the other hand, is more specifically defined as a cooperative process in which two or more people work together toward a shared goal, leveraging their collective expertise, resources, and effort. It isn't simply working in the same proximity or group. It encompasses an interdependence to achieve high-level outcomes that could not be accomplished individually. Collaboration takes focus, intentionality, and effort.

People sometimes believe that if you take a group of high-performers, Collaboration will happen naturally. In reality, this is not the case. Research from HBR shows that without a focus on Collaboration, complex teams are less likely to share knowledge freely, learn from one another, flexibly shift workloads, help one another, or share resources.[67]

One of the most interesting studies that drives this point home is the super chicken experiment.[68] Conducted by biologist William Muir, this study looked at the difference between a coop of all high-producing chickens (called "super chickens") and an average coop of poultry. Surprisingly, the average chickens ended up producing more eggs than the super chickens. It was found that the super chicken coop had excessive competition and aggression among the hens and, therefore, produced fewer eggs. What do chickens have to do with people? This study highlights that just putting high-performers together is not enough to create extraordinary teams and organizations.

In executive teams, the same dynamic can play out. When everyone's trying to win individually, the group loses collectively. Your job as CEO is to build a system that rewards Collaboration over competition. If you're wondering where your team sits on this journey, ask: Are we a group of high-performers or a high-performing team?

Collaboration is essential for bringing people together in a meaningful way and solving complex problems. In today's fast-paced and variable environment, deliberately prioritizing Collaboration is essential. Teams and organizations are faced with even more complexity given increasing economic pressure, hybrid work environments, and ever-changing technology. Effective Collaboration is key for achieving organizational goals, but teams often struggle with working together, holding each other accountable, or maintaining high performance. A meta-analysis in healthcare that included 31 studies composed of 1,390 teams showed the importance of Collaboration in team performance. The teams with strong Collaboration, regardless of size, were nearly three times more likely to achieve better outcomes than those without it.[69]

Collaboration is equally important at the broader organizational level. Too often, departments are siloed in organizations without leveraging one another to achieve results for the company. A *Forbes* article explains that cross-department Collaboration is "the practice of different departments within an organization working together toward a common goal."[70] This article highlights that cross-department Collaboration fosters greater innovation, shared knowledge, continuous learning, increased agility, and more effective achievement of complex business goals. To ensure companies benefit from the positive outcomes of Collaboration, they must concentrate on three key areas: team support, accountability, and excellence. Let's take a closer look at each of these.

Team Support

Team support refers to the willingness and consistency of people to go beyond their roles to aid their colleagues. Extensive research highlights the pivotal role of team support in enhancing team effectiveness and performance outcomes.[71] Team support includes several concepts like information sharing, social support, and task support. It is simply asking: Do we help one another succeed?

People are wired to work together and help each other. We have a tribal instinct that is deeply ingrained, and when it is leveraged productively, it helps to create supportive, inclusive environments where we all can thrive. When teams are highly supportive, everyone is more likely to meet both individual and team goals. The potential for each employee to become much greater than they would have been alone is exponential.

One of the most meaningful steps to creating a culture of team support is understanding one another's strengths. It is hard to lean on someone else when you are not clear on how you can do so. Taking the steps to understand each other's strengths and ways of thinking can be a great way to understand the best ways to support each other. One of the greatest barriers to team support is the misperception that asking for someone's help is a burden or shows weakness. We tend to hold back, telling ourselves excuses, such as . . .

The other person's plate is too full.

I don't want to be a burden.

It feels too vulnerable.

I can do everything myself.
I don't need help.

These assumptions are incorrect—they're flawed narratives we tell ourselves. The truth is, you *can't* do it all, and you *do* need help. Most people want to help us succeed, and assisting others fosters well-being. Think about the last time someone asked you for help. How did it make you feel?

Building an environment where people ask for and are willing to offer help creates the greatest access for team support. In a team environment, we sometimes believe that we need to have all the answers, excel at everything, and hide our own opportunities for growth. These are misperceptions as well. When team members all try to operate independently, team support suffers, and the work produced is inefficient. A team where helping each other is the norm optimizes team members' strengths, creating allyship where everyone lifts each other up and supports each other's best selves. Moreover, when teams support each other, their members aren't as prone to burnout due to taking on too much themselves.

Team support also applies more broadly at the organizational level. When cross-functional teams support one another, share information and resources, and help each other succeed, the ultimate outcome is increased customer experiences. We can all recall instances in our lives where this hasn't happened. Think of a time when you were bounced around from one help desk to another, with everyone insisting it wasn't their department. This reflects the consequences of teams within organizations failing to support one another effectively. We can do better, and it is essential that we strive for improvement.

Fostering team support throughout the organization is one essential ingredient in how we get there.

Taking Action: Team Support

As I have shared throughout this book, understanding each other's strengths and personality preferences builds team cohesion and organizational culture. Having the right tools with the right conversations is essential. Teams have an increased ability to support one another when they understand each other, know how to work together more effectively, and can lean on each other's strengths.

When I work with teams, I often share that we work more on the *how* and less on the *what*. This means 99 percent of our time in the business world is focused on our results, our work products, and what we are producing. My coaching is focused on how we accomplish that by working together. The *what* at this level will always be complex and challenging, but it gets easier by optimizing how we do "the hard stuff" together.

Understanding each other's personality preferences is incredibly beneficial for teams. No matter what tool I used, it led to a good discussion about how to work effectively together. However, until I met the team at Principles, I felt a bit stuck between my academic community and the business world on this.

Many of the personality tools on the market that are very popular in the business world are based on outdated psychological science. So I went on a quest to find a personality assessment that was not only based on the most up-to-date science but also created advancements in team cohesion and culture and was easy to interpret without a psychologist leading the way. It was a tall order, for sure. I looked at assessment after assessment and either felt they lacked the reliability and validity I needed, or they were so complex that ease of use was an issue. After a year and a half of searching, a colleague asked if I had heard of the new company Principles. I had not, but I quickly started researching them.

I learned that Principles had been founded to bring evidence-based tools into businesses to help enhance culture and team performance. The company had originated as an offshoot of Bridgewater, the well-known investment company led by Ray Dalio. Bridgewater had been recognized for its strong culture and emphasis on transparency, candor, and feedback. Zack Wieder, the CEO of Principles, had served as the former Head of Culture at Bridgewater. Ray and Zack had established Principles to provide other organizations with the opportunity to leverage the robust toolset they had developed as the backbone of the Bridgewater culture.

The Principles team has created tools that are scientifically backed and easy for businesses to access and use. They were developed in collaboration with leading experts like Dr. Brian Little, a renowned personality psychologist, and Dr. Adam Grant, an organizational psychologist and bestselling author. When I explored their personality assessment, it felt like the clouds parted and the sun was shining. My long search was finally over! I had discovered the tool I had been seeking.

The PrinciplesUs Personality Assessment is valid, reliable, grounded in current personality science, easily interpretable, and enhances teams and organizational culture. PrinciplesUs is the gold standard of personality tools, helping teams and organizations excel across the 5Cs. The assessment and platform help teams build the self-awareness and mutual understanding essential for great Collaboration. By surfacing thinking preferences, motivators, and working styles, the tool fosters empathy and mutual understanding and improves communication. The interactive platform allows individuals to gain self-awareness by understanding their strengths and preferences while also providing insights into team composition and dynamics. All of these elements are essential for team support.

Another action you can take is to foster a culture of asking for help—and yes, you as the leader must go first. But it takes practice. A simple way to start is by asking yourself: What's one thing I could lean on others for?

Here are two additional strategies to help you practice asking for help to foster a culture of team support.

- **Engage others in your development.** It's powerful to engage others because you are accomplishing many things at once: asking for help, being vulnerable, building trust, and acknowledging others' strengths.
- **Lead a helping circle exercise with your team.** Schedule time in a group setting where each person asks for help and shares one area where they need support. As the leader, you will go first to model asking for help. If you aren't requesting assistance, no one else will. Ask each person in the group to respond to the following prompts:
  - You can lean on me for . . .
  - I need to lean on others for . . .

Allow team members to raise their hands and respond: "I can help you with that."

Knowledge sharing also creates more team support. One way to accomplish this is by establishing a shared repository of information and resources, leveraging existing platforms if possible. Next, consider what would benefit the team and, ultimately, the organization. It is also worthwhile to take time in a team meeting to discuss what information is currently shared, what's working, and what could be improved. This can also be a topic for cross-functional teams to explore better ways to share information and resources with one another. And it helps people hold each other accountable.

Accountability

Accountability measures the commitment to holding individuals and groups within the organization responsible for their performance in a fair and consistent manner. Similarly, accountability research underscores its critical impact on various aspects of team and organizational performance, including team trust, commitment, efficacy, task performance, and team identification.[72]

I cannot count how many times I have heard leaders say that they need more accountability from their team and organization. It is sometimes more about another 5Cs subfactor than actual accountability. At its core, accountability is about taking ownership of our actions, decisions, and behaviors and holding others accountable for the same. When we are accountable, we are committed to our goals and follow through on our commitments.

If accountability is so critical, why do we struggle with it? For example, why do 80 percent of people give up on their New Year's resolutions one month into the year after they have made the commitment?[73] Interestingly, research shows that accountability is significantly higher when it involves interpersonal interactions, such as partnerships or group settings, rather than relying solely on individual efforts. A study by the Association for Talent Development found that individuals who commit to someone else about their goals have a 65 percent chance of achieving them, and the probability increases to 95 percent when they engage in regular check-ins with an accountability partner.[74]

Given this data, teams and organizational settings are ideal environments for accountability, with plenty of partners available. Yet accountability still seems to be a pain point for many leaders and teams. The 5Cs Model and the layering of the rings give us insight into why this could be. Accountability is maximized when the Candid Communication ring is optimized. Leveraging one another in accountability requires open, honest feedback loops, especially when we are not keeping our commitments.

The highest-performing teams hold each other accountable and don't solely rely on the leader to set performance standards. Teams that are not accountable to each other often use triangulation with the leader to solve their issues. This ends up wasting the leader's time, breaking down trust, and leading to lower team performance. In fast-paced environments, it can feel easier to just loop in the leader rather than pause to address something peer-to-peer. And in cultures where hierarchy is deeply ingrained, people may not even feel it's their place to hold a colleague accountable. As Steve Gruenert and Todd Whitaker wrote in *School Culture Rewired*, "The culture of any organization is shaped by the worst behavior the leader is willing to tolerate." While their focus was on schools, the insight is universal: What leaders ignore becomes a form of unspoken permission. This is why accountability isn't just structural, it's cultural.[75]

Changing that mindset takes intention, consistency, and modeling from the top. This applies to the broader organization as well. Think for a moment about the difference between peers across teams and departments holding each other accountable versus running directly to the leader of that department. A culture of universal accountability encourages people to take ownership and to be willing to identify issues and discuss them openly. It minimizes the lag time between identifying and discussing problems. Taking steps to build universal accountability is essential for building optimal teams and organizational culture.

Universal and team accountability can be hard. As CEO, your organization's accountability system starts with what you model—and what you're willing to confront. Silence around misalignment is a form of approval. True accountability requires courage and a foundation of Candid Communication. Many avoid it, because direct conversations about accountability can feel risky or uncomfortable. Others struggle because they haven't clearly defined expectations in the first place.

Accountability can also be confused with blame, but they're fundamentally different. Accountability is forward-looking; it's about ownership, learning, and taking responsibility to improve outcomes. Blame, on the other hand, is backward-facing. It focuses on fault, often driven by fear or frustration, and tends to shut down learning. Blame discourages; true accountability empowers.

Taking Action: Accountability

One of the most successful ways teams can increase accountability is through collective goal setting with the associated rewards. When you create goals that are not singular but rather collective, you incentivize more accountability through structure and rewards. Most businesses excel at creating meaningful goals, yet creating common or shared goals is what is needed to increase accountability. Using frameworks like SMART (specific, measurable, achievable, relevant, time-bound) goals helps to clarify the objective at the right level.[76] Current research in goal setting emphasizes the importance of goals being both specific and challenging in nature.[77]

SMART goals are first introduced in the Clarity ring as a tool to set shared goals, but Clarity alone isn't enough. When applied intentionally, SMART goals also drive accountability by creating shared ownership and structure around what needs to get done, by when, and by whom. In the context of accountability, SMART goals do more than clarify, they also operationalize follow-through. When goals are specific, time-bound, and collectively owned, it becomes easier to track progress, celebrate wins, and have honest conversations when commitments are missed. In this way, SMART goals become a mutual commitment tool, making expectations explicit and reinforcing a culture of shared responsibility. This doesn't mean there aren't single points of ownership for tasks. It means there's Clarity around collective goals and visibility into who owns what.

SMART Goals Quick Guide

Use this framework to set clear, actionable goals that drive success.

Goal Statement: Define your goal clearly.

SMART Breakdown

- **Specific:** What exactly do you want to achieve?
- **Measurable:** How will you track progress?
- **Achievable:** Is this realistic given your resources?
- **Relevant:** Does this align with your broader objectives?
- **Time-bound:** What's your deadline?

Action Steps

Step 1: ________________ Deadline: ____ Ownership: _____
Step 2: ________________ Deadline: ____ Ownership: _____
Step 3: ________________ Deadline: ____ Ownership: _____

Success Indicators

How will you know you've achieved your goal?

Cross-functional goals take accountability to an even higher level and help people get into the "one company" mindset. Cross-functional project teams can be utilized to solve critical organizational challenges or drive important initiatives. It is an incredible way to get people across the organization to build relationships, bring a diversity of perspectives together, and unify goals that align the organization. By taking a strategic approach to cross-functional project teams and goals, organizations can enhance accountability, productivity, and overall culture. People work together for shared results that ultimately have a deep and wide impact across the organization while holding one another accountable.

With a focus on the 5Cs, cross-functional teams can become a true asset for the organization. One of the major subfactors of the 5Cs involving accountability is psychological safety. A common question that arises is whether a psychologically safe environment allows us to forgo holding people accountable or maintaining high standards. The answer is a resounding NO. These are distinct continuums that have equal importance. The synergy of accountability and psychological safety is what fosters an organization toward a learning culture that aims for excellence instead of perfection.

Excellence

Excellence refers to the drive toward high performance, the rejection of mediocrity, and the desire to learn from mistakes. Moreover, striving for excellence within teams is essential as it cultivates a culture of continuous improvement, fosters innovation, and ultimately contributes to overall organizational performance.[78] As CEO, it's your job to define what excellence looks like, model it consistently, and create the conditions for others to rise to that standard, but it's critical to remember that striving for excellence is not the same as chasing perfection.

> “Success depends on high standards, not being flawless. The target is not perfection—it's excellence.”
>
> —Adam Grant[79]

Studies have shown that when people strive for excellence instead of perfection, they achieve greater results. Teams that celebrate wins and learn from failures are 25 times as likely to be successful in the long term.[80] Unfortunately, many of us are perfectionists (or recovering ones) who are scared to death of any type of failure. Striving for perfection versus excellence creates a fear-based culture, where mistakes aren't allowed and the culture lacks psychological safety, which impedes innovation. This applies at both the team and organizational level.

Edmondson has done incredible work in helping people understand the continuum of failure. She explains that failure takes many different forms, but that too often we go to extremes in our minds. On the right side of her continuum is productive failure, including exploratory testing and hypothesis testing. This is the space where science and innovation live, and failure is about learning. In the middle of the continuum is failure stemming from uncertainty, process complexity, and challenges. This is the place where you need to ask questions about why something failed or WHAT caused it (not who). The left side of the continuum is failure resulting from deviance or inattention.[81] This type of failure usually requires a one-on-one coaching conversation and is focused on the WHO.

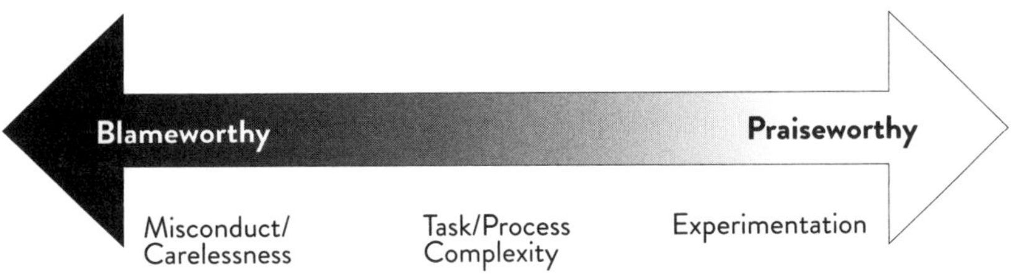

Adapted from Amy Edmondson's Framework on Types of Failure

The reason I share this continuum is that we very rarely separate the concept of failure into different categories. We tend to label all failure as negative when that is truly not the case. We shy away from learning conversations that can help organizations grow optimally and get better every year. A key to high-performing teams and thriving cultures is to shift your mindset away from perfection and understand that celebrating our imperfections is essential to becoming a learning, agile organization.

There is an ancient Japanese philosophy called wabi-sabi, a concept that asks us to search for the beauty in imperfection. Kintsugi, in which broken objects are repaired with liquid gold, giving them "golden scars," is a traditional art form that comes from wabi-sabi. The practice celebrates the cracks. Why? Cracks build resilience, and that's what makes us beautiful. Instead of hiding the imperfections, they are celebrated. This reflects a wabi-sabi mindset—one that values imperfection as a natural part of being human. It encourages us to recognize and appreciate our "cracks," understanding that Connection isn't built on perfection, but on our shared humanity.

Think of a time when someone told you about their flawless success . . . and another time when someone told you a story about how they overcame a setback, learned from it, and then succeeded. Which one resonated more deeply with you?

The wabi-sabi mindset allows you and those around you to let go of the unproductive (and impossible) pursuit of perfectionism. Taking time to reflect on lessons learned from failures, whether individually or with your team, fosters psychological safety through vulnerability and promotes a growth mindset. Within an organization, it nurtures a learning culture grounded in both psychological safety and high standards. A learning culture embraces a growth mindset, encouraging everyone to move out of their comfort zones and into their learning and growth zones on a regular basis.

Covara Creates a Wabi-Sabi Practice

Lena knew Covara was classically in the category of saying "Everything is awesome" but failing financially. The company had tried multiple versions of retrospectives, from lessons learned to postmortems (of course, no one wants to engage in a process with that name) to roses and thorns. However, they had not adopted a consistent practice or culture of learning. In fact, when I started working with Lena, I wasn't even allowed to use the word *failure* in any of my materials for the company.

Lena and I decided to try something completely different and use the science of positive psychology to craft the process and questions, with wabi-sabi as the central principle. It was rolled out first with the executive leadership team, then quickly gained traction in Rachel's marketing organization. Then it went viral and was adopted company-wide. Covara now regularly uses this practice to help their people reflect, grow, and learn.

Taking Action: Excellence

Creating a wabi-sabi practice in your organization can make a huge difference for your team and company. Here are the steps you can take to cultivate this.

1. **Create the space to pause.**

   It is so easy to get caught up in the busyness of business. To learn from failures, first take time to pause. Integrating "learning from doing" with "learning from pausing and reflecting" offers numerous benefits: It improves self-efficacy, increases self-awareness, develops creative thinking skills, and boosts performance.[82] As leaders, we can help create the space for reflecting on both successes and, especially, failures. Pausing provides an opportunity to clarify what happened in the situation versus who was involved. Without pausing, we often create stories—since humans are storytelling machines—without considering the facts. By distinguishing the facts from the stories, we gain a better understanding of what occurred and move away from blaming one another.

2. **Go beyond the surface in reflective conversations.**

   As you review the facts, highlight both the strengths and areas of improvement. Consider what was imperfect about the situation with kindness and compassion. When we look at successes and failures, we often view them as binary: Either it was a complete success or an utter failure. A more holistic way to view failure is on Edmondson's continuum. Most of the time, when a situation or project breaks down or fails, it falls within the middle of the continuum. This could be because of process issues or complexity, task challenges, or uncertainty. Recognizing that there's a range within failure can help as you process the situation.

3. **Focus on discovering the wisdom.**
   The way you repair what's imperfect with gold is to discover the wisdom in what's flawed. What can you learn from the projects or situations that didn't go the way you planned? As you reflect, incorporate where your challenge or setback falls on the failure continuum. For situations that fall on the blameworthy side, you might privately ask for coaching or, for someone on your team, coach and develop them. For situations that fall in the middle, explore what broke down in the process or situation and how it could be improved. For situations that fall on the praiseworthy side of the spectrum, discover what you learned from the undesired result and how you could use that to expand your knowledge.

Collaboration is essential for high-performing teams and thriving organizational cultures. It is the factor that brings diverse individuals together into a cohesive team capable of achieving exceptional results. Through team support, people are strengthened and help each other grow. Accountability helps teams cultivate a culture of ownership, uphold their commitments, and drive collective progress. Finally, the pursuit of excellence versus perfection helps teams and organizations maintain high standards and cultivate a learning culture capable of agility, innovation, and growth. By nurturing Collaboration and its subfactors, you unlock the full potential of people, creating not just a culture of performance but one of shared success.

Key Takeaways

Collaboration encompasses interdependence to achieve high-level outcomes that could not be achieved individually. It takes focus, intentionality, and effort.

Team support refers to the willingness and consistency of people to go beyond their roles to aid and support their colleagues. A great first step to increase team support is learning about each other's strengths and personality preferences through a tool like the PrinciplesUs Personality Assessment.

Accountability measures the commitment to holding individuals and groups within the organization responsible for their performance in a fair and consistent manner. A key to increasing accountability within teams and organizations is collective goal setting using frameworks like SMART.

Strive for excellence rather than perfection. This will enable a learning culture that leads to more innovation and performance. Consider using the wabi-sabi methodology to promote more retrospectives in your team and organization.

Main Barriers to Overcome

Perfectionism: We fall into the perfection trap and forget that Collaboration is fundamentally about learning. High-performing teams can mistakenly equate Collaboration with flawless execution—expecting every interaction to be smooth and every contribution to be polished. But real Collaboration is messy. It requires learning in public, sharing unfinished ideas, making mistakes, and iterating in real time. When teams chase perfection, they avoid the very discomfort that leads to insight, growth, and excellence.

Discomfort: We avoid holding each other accountable because it feels uncomfortable. True Collaboration isn't just about supporting one another; it's about expecting the best from each other. Holding someone accountable for their commitments or calling out a drop in standards can feel risky for the relationship. But when teams avoid these conversations, leaders carry the burden alone, and the team loses a critical driver of performance and shared ownership.

CHAPTER 6

Contribution

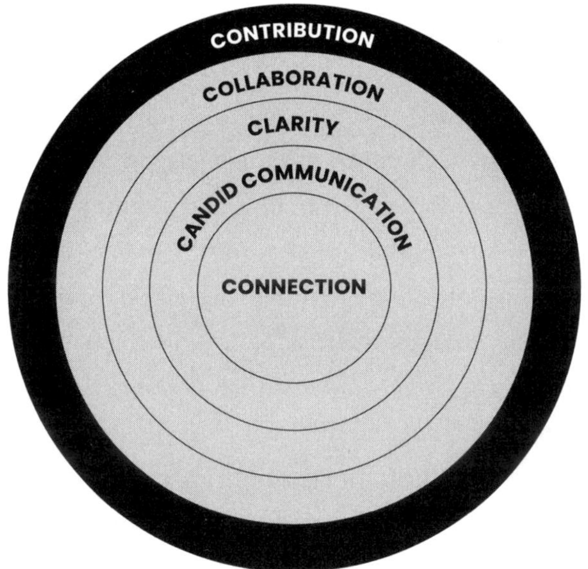

As a foundation for Covara's cultural transformation, the company conducted a company-wide 5Cs Culture assessment to establish a baseline of their strengths and opportunities. When they received their results, they found that their strongest factor was actually Contribution. Employees felt a strong connection to the vision and core values, experienced a sense of meaning and importance, and recognized the impact the company was making on the communities and stakeholders they served. The company's greatest opportunity lay in strengthening the

psychological safety of their culture. The steps they took to achieve this serve as a road map for any organization looking to enhance their 5Cs.

First and foremost, Lena openly shared the survey results with the entire organization in a town hall meeting, emphasizing the leadership team's commitment to making meaningful change. She highlighted the organization's cultural strengths in Contribution and their greatest opportunity for growth in psychological safety. Lena emphasized the importance of not trying to address everything all at once but being clear and intentional in positively moving the needle on psychological safety. She articulated the plan to do so with Dave, their Chief Culture Officer, leading the way.

The first step in the plan was to provide people across the company with the resources to strengthen their understanding of psychological safety and the behaviors that could positively impact it. Far too often, cultural initiatives are communicated via online training that seems more like a check-the-box exercise instead of a true opportunity for growth. Covara was committed to ensuring their journey was meaningful and impactful, not an exercise in futility.

They started a cultural ambassador program that included 120 cross-functional people at every level in the organization. These cultural ambassadors, along with the top 200 leaders, became an organized coalition for change and were given the tools and training to lead conversations to enhance psychological safety. A one-pager with specific actions people could take, including questions that helped build psychological safety, was distributed company-wide. Psychological safety was also integrated into leadership development programs across the company, and a central repository for resources was created for anyone to access. A steady drumbeat of the importance of this continued in all communications throughout the year, along with a continued focus on their core values and the behaviors that enhanced psychological safety. Culture is a strategic priority for Covara, so every leader was required to set goals around it and have a defined road map for how to achieve them.

Contribution Creates Fulfillment

Contribution, the final factor, encompasses impact, core values, meaning and mattering, and shared vision. It is the factor through which we see people get the deepest levels of fulfillment from their work. We spend two-thirds of our waking hours at work, so being intentional about feeling fulfilled in our professional life is paramount. People sometimes refer to companies as "families." While this statement can be misleading and off-putting to some, thinking of our places of work as communities is more on point. When businesses operate as a community of connected human beings supporting each other and working toward creating their greatest Contribution, they have unlimited potential.

People increasingly confirm that they want to work within a culture where they can thrive. The opportunity to turn our businesses into thriving communities has never been greater. A 2023 report from Gallup shared that people were seeking new job opportunities at the highest rate since 2015, while overall satisfaction with their company had hit a record low.[83] In 2024, American employees' connection to their companies' missions and purposes was at an all-time low of only 30 percent.[84]

It is our responsibility as leaders within organizations to reverse this negative trend and emphasize the crucial aspect of Contribution. It reflects how people's beliefs and actions align with the organization's core values, purpose, impact, and sense of meaning and mattering to their team and organization. It incorporates the impact of the team and organization on the broader community, the existence and acceptance of key core values that drive actions and discussions, the recognition of meaning and mattering, and the creation of company-wide alignment on a shared vision that provides organizational direction and purpose.

Contribution is optimized through every other 5Cs factor. It drives organizational performance, directly impacts engagement and morale, and leads to a positive work environment where people feel seen, heard, and valued. Research in both positive organizational psychology and organizational psychology consistently highlights the importance of people feeling a connection to purpose and meaningful work to increase satisfaction, motivation, commitment, and performance.[85] A first step in optimizing this factor requires teams and organizations to have a shared vision and purpose.

Shared Vision and Purpose

Shared vision refers to the alignment and commitment of all members to a unified direction and purpose. Research shows that a strong vision significantly influences team performance, as organizations with a clear purpose and direction demonstrate better future performance.[86] There seems to be a lot of confusion about the difference between vision, mission, and purpose statements. So let's put some definitions around these as a starting point.

- **VISION** is the picture. It's **where** you will be one day or what you aspire to do.

- **MISSION** is the road map to get there. It's **what** you do to accomplish your purpose and what drives you to get there.
- **PURPOSE** is the feeling that everyone experiences when they accomplish their goals. It's **why** you exist; it is the reason you are doing what you are doing and what guides you. It speaks to your impact on customers, employees, and partners.

These ideas are often used interchangeably in organizations, but they are separate and distinct. However, combining one or more of them can be useful if it works for your organization.

A shared vision is critical because it acts as a unifying force, aligning people within a team or organization. It can also anchor people to a collective sense of identity and belonging that helps them thrive. It serves as a constant source of motivation that inspires action. A strong vision can encourage people to think innovatively, embrace change, and continually drive for results. However, it doesn't emerge organically. As CEO, you have to name it, repeat it, and model it daily. If you don't build that narrative, someone else will—and misalignment will follow.

Research from *Forbes* that collected data from over 50,000 people showed that when employees connect to the company's vision, they are significantly more engaged at work.[87] This North Star can also enhance external perceptions of the company to attract top talent who resonate with the company's purpose and vision. Whether you are creating the company vision for the first time, refreshing an existing one, or communicating a well-defined one, taking action to enhance this subfactor is vital for creating a thriving team and culture.

Taking Action: Shared Vision and Purpose

If you are creating a vision and purpose statement for the first time, it should harness the collective wisdom of the organization and not solely focus on the perspective of leadership. The word *shared* in this subfactor is there for a reason. When people can see themselves, their interests, and their purpose in the statement, they can easily be on the same page and move in an aligned direction.

A key to creating a vision statement is simplicity. Far too often, these statements become jumbled with so many words that no one can remember them. As I shared previously, language is instrumental in shaping culture, and you want people to be able to easily recite the company's North Star.

Consider for a moment: Are there any iconic company visions that you can easily recite? If so, why? It's probably because they are straightforward and evoke both a thought and an emotional response. Here are some examples:

- Microsoft: "We empower the world"[88]
- Whole Foods: "To nourish people and the planet"[89]
- IKEA: "To create a better everyday life for the many people"[90]

These clear statements help to create organizational alignment and ultimately drive culture.

If you already have a statement, whether it's a refreshed version or newly created, there's nothing more powerful than stories to help people connect with it. We spend much of our corporate lives focused on sharing analytics and data, often going to extremes that can best be described as death by PowerPoint. Far too often, we see slides packed with so many words, figures, and charts that no one can absorb the full context.

Storytelling is an underused motivational tool for connecting people to concepts and, most importantly, to a company's vision and purpose. By engaging both the cognitive and emotional centers of the brain, it is one of the most powerful ways to help people connect emotionally and remember key messages. People have been telling stories since the beginning of time to pass down concepts through human experiences. It can bridge the gap between knowledge and understanding, logic and emotion, and information and action. The more you communicate the company's vision and purpose, the better. However, your behaviors and actions need to align consistently with this North Star. One way to further define how you do this is through clarity in the team and organizational core values.

Core Values

Defining core values and integrating them into daily actions, discussions, and decisions creates the company's internal compass. Research from Finegan[91] and Jin and Drozdenko[92] demonstrated that clarity and integration of organizational values into daily actions and discussions fosters higher levels of commitment and performance. Further research from Qualtrics in 2022 showed that when people felt alignment with their company's mission, vision, and values, they were two and half times more likely to say that their work gave them a sense of personal accomplishment, and over half (56 percent) would not even consider a job at a company if they did not agree with its values.[93]

Defining core values is foundational, but without understanding how they translate to behaviors, they risk being merely words on a wall or website.

On the surface, language may seem simple. However, when you pause to recognize how many different meanings and interpretations words can have, you realize how critical it is to define each word in a core value. Take, for example, the word *teamwork*. As I shared previously, we aren't defining teamwork solely as collaboration, even though that is the case in many publications.

The next step is to clarify what each core value means and what it doesn't. For example, a company I once worked with chose the word *grit* as a core value. They defined it in alignment with Angela Duckworth's research in this area as "perseverance and passion for long-term goals."[94] Without defining behaviors around this value, it could be interpreted that this organization wanted their employees to get things done at all costs. That was not the intention at all. In fact, the organization deeply valued the well-being of its people. To help their staff understand this core value, they went on to clearly define the behaviors so everyone would know how to embody them. This step was critical for people to understand how to integrate the company and team values into their everyday actions.

Defining core values is also an essential step in developing an organization's culture; they set the foundation, guide decision-making, and help align people's behavior with its mission. Edgar Schein, one of the leading experts in organizational culture, explains that core values are foundational in shaping an organization's culture and provide a framework for understanding how values influence behavior and performance.[95] Research in organizational psychology and the business world continually shows that organizations with clear values are more successful at fostering engagement, ethical behavior, and alignment with strategic goals, all of which contribute to better performance. For example, Dr. Kim Cameron's research showed that companies with a cohesive culture aligned with core values can better sustain performance, adapt to change, and foster high levels of motivation, leading to improved organizational outcomes.[96]

Taking Action: Core Values

Defining core values can be an incredible team-building, connecting, and energizing experience at the team and organizational level. I usually start with the C-suite team, using several methodologies to guide the discussion. My goal when facilitating this conversation is to help people consider the essential words and feel their significance. I use The Visual Explorer deck from the Center for Creative Leadership with 500 photographs from around the world and a core values deck with words as tools.[97] I ask participants to look at the pictures and words and choose three that they believe represent critical representations of who they are as a team or company and who they aspire to be.

A question that comes up often is whether our core values are aspirational or who we are currently. Different philosophies exist, but combining both can be the most powerful. Once we have discussed the three ideas from each person, we land on the top three to five as group and then further define them and their associated behaviors. This is just the beginning of our work together, however, because this conversation only represents ideas from the top leadership team and not the broader organization.

The next step is to ensure the organization actively participates in cultivating these core values. This can be done in several ways. I have seen great success with listening groups throughout the organization at every level, using technology platforms to gather feedback, and empowering leadership teams with the resources they need to collect their team's input. Once you have gathered enough information, you can proceed with the final crafting and communication of the core values and behaviors.

If your company has already defined its core values, but they are not truly a compass for your desired culture, I encourage a refresh and recommitment through one of the methodologies I shared.

Defining core values makes invisible aspects of culture broadly visible so everyone understands how to flourish within the organization. The next step is to intentionally demonstrate the company values with every opportunity and continuously integrate them within the organization, from leadership development to rewards and recognition to daily communication.

Impact

Impact refers to the emphasis on generating meaningful outcomes that benefit stakeholders and the wider community. In 2007, Adam Grant conducted a study that beautifully highlighted the importance of people understanding their impact to enhance performance. The study was conducted in a university's call center, where employees were responsible for soliciting alumni donations to fund student scholarships. The call center was chosen because there was a pervasive disconnect between the work itself and its impact. The control group received no intervention, another group was told how their work could benefit them personally (for example, financial bonuses or personal job satisfaction), and the final group was introduced to a scholarship recipient who shared how the funds had made a real difference in their education and future opportunities.

One month later, the group exposed to the scholarship recipient saw a dramatic increase in performance compared to the other groups. They spent 142 percent more time on the phone with potential donors and achieved a 171 percent increase in generated revenue. As expected, the control group that had received no additional information showed no change in their performance. The biggest surprise was that the group receiving personal benefit information also showed no change in their performance.[98] This study highlights the importance of individuals understanding how their work affects customers and stakeholders.

Far too often, people feel removed from the impact of their work, which can lead to a lack of motivation and disconnection from the company. Placing the customer at the center of every conversation, decision, and action can help employees shift their mindsets to view their work through an impact lens. People are prone to getting stuck in accomplishing their tasks without thinking more broadly about the potential impacts of their work. A crucial role for leaders is to help people consistently connect their own and their team's efforts to the ultimate customer or stakeholder. At times, this involves fostering internal connections between departments to demonstrate how everything is interlinked. When people don't understand how their work fits in, silos can form, resulting in a lack of ownership necessary to drive customer results. Shifting the focus to prioritize impact is crucial for maximizing team performance and enhancing organizational culture.

Taking Action: Impact

The greatest action organizations can take in this area is connecting employees to the people they impact. This can be done in multiple ways, such as finding opportunities to bring customers in for discussions, panels, and focus groups or encouraging employees who aren't typically in the field to branch out. For example, a person in finance may not get to see their work's everyday impact, so creating opportunities for this can enhance their motivation and performance. Invite someone from the front line to a finance team meeting to share a real story of how a timely invoice, budget approval, or funding decision made a difference for a customer. A hospital financial analyst may learn how budget planning enables critical care delivery.

You can also use storytelling by regularly sharing customer stories in communications, videos, and testimonials. Keeping feedback loops open between the organization and the customer and then sharing that data with employees can also help them stay connected. For example, the use of customer feedback tools like Net Promoter Scores (NPS) or stakeholder feedback, along with qualitative comments, can keep people informed about customer outcomes.

Incorporating understanding impact into leadership development programs through shadowing customer-facing roles, participating in customer innovation initiatives, and conducting customer research are a few examples of additional actions. The right mix of opportunities will depend on your industry and company, but prioritizing this is essential for improvement in this subfactor. Taking action in the Impact subfactor can also enhance people's sense of meaning and mattering.

Meaning and Mattering

Meaning and mattering refer to the recognition and sense of value of each individual's Contribution to the team and organization. Research highlights the critical importance of feeling a sense of meaning and mattering at work, as it significantly correlates with higher levels of work engagement, commitment, job satisfaction, life satisfaction, performance, and general well-being; it is also inversely related to withdrawal intentions and negative affect.[99]

When people feel that their work isn't meaningful or recognized within the company, they become disengaged. In 2022, the U.S. Surgeon General released a "Framework for Workplace Mental Health & Well-Being" that included "Mattering at Work" as one of the six components. This report explained that this component "rests on the human needs of dignity and meaning. Dignity is the sense of being respected and valued." The report further noted that meaning referred to the "sense of broader purpose and significance of one's work."[100]

As I have shared, people have a fundamental need to be seen, heard, and acknowledged. This applies to *all* people, not just some. Focusing on meaning and mattering at the team and organizational level helps people thrive mentally, physically, and emotionally.

Organizational psychologist Zach Mercurio describes this subfactor simply as "I am valued, and I add value." The impact subfactor can be explained as "The company adds value."[101] Of course, these subfactors are intrinsically linked. One of the most powerful ways to enhance people's sense of meaning and mattering is to focus on both recognition and appreciation. That said, HBR reported that 59 percent of people said they had never had a boss who "truly appreciates" them, and 53 percent admitted they would stay longer at their company if they felt more appreciated for their work.[102]

While recognition and appreciation may seem the same at first glance, they are slightly different.

- **Recognition** is tied to someone's performance or results. It is focused on their accomplishments.
- **Appreciation** is more focused on the person for who they are and their efforts, qualities, or contributions, regardless of specific outcomes. It emphasizes gratitude for the person's *being* rather than their *doing*.

In other words, recognition is for *doing*. Appreciation is for *being*. In the workplace, we tend to overfocus on recognition without enough emphasis on appreciation. Most teams overindex on the former and underinvest in the latter. Finding a balance can go a long way toward helping employees feel fully acknowledged. Solely focusing on recognition can foster an environment where accomplishment is valued for validation. To express the importance of both being and doing, intentionally appreciate people's inherent value just as much as you recognize them for their achievements. Take action on this subfactor by raising awareness of how you can balance recognition and appreciation, creating an intentional focus on gratitude and strengths.

Taking Action: Meaning and Mattering

One of my favorite ways to cultivate more meaning and mattering across a team and organization was inspired by Shawn Achor's concept of the "Prism of Praise."[103] This activity can be done with small teams or in a room of hundreds—even virtually. If conducted in person, start by cutting large sticky flip chart paper in half vertically and taping one half-sheet to each participant's back like a cape. Give everyone a marker, and for the next 15 minutes, invite participants to walk around the room and write one strength or positive quality they genuinely see in each person directly on their "cape." Encourage brief but meaningful comments—just a word or short phrase—so participants can connect with as many others as possible during the time. By the end of the exercise, each person will have a cape filled with the strengths that others see in them, a powerful, tangible reminder of their impact. To adapt this virtually, assign each person a slide or digital whiteboard space and ask participants to write strengths on one another's boards during a timed reflection. No matter the format, it is an opportunity for teams large and small to appreciate each other. It also creates Connection and a deep sense of meaning and mattering. You can do several simpler exercises with similar results, like ending a meeting by acknowledging the person next to you or simply with a moment of gratitude. All of these practices create positive emotions and inspire deeper Connection, action, and well-being.

Expressing gratitude toward others is something we must focus on and be intentional about. An HBR study found that the more power a leader has at work, the less gratitude they are likely to feel and express.[104] One reason is that those expressing gratitude underestimate its positive impact on the receiver. Writing down three things you are grateful for every day greatly enhances your well-being. If these statements are directed toward others, it can also increase their sense of meaning and mattering.

The hardest yet most important action you can take is to start with yourself. I know you might want to skip this paragraph, but please hear me out. We tend to be incredibly negative toward ourselves; this is partly due to our biases. If anyone else treated us the way we treat ourselves, we would probably label them as toxic. Cultivating a best friendship with yourself through gratitude and appreciation can greatly benefit you and enhance your ability to appreciate others. It's also a wonderful way to continuously counteract negativity bias. You can begin with these two simple questions:

- What do I appreciate about myself?
- What gratitude could I express toward myself?

Don't worry if this feels completely unnatural at first. Keep doing it, and one day it will become easier.

Covara's Incredible Results

Six months after the initial 5Cs survey, the company assessed its progress using a subset of the data to verify that the initiatives were indeed making a difference. The results indicated substantial progress, with an overall increase of 20 percent in psychological safety. The company remained focused and committed to its plan and journey for the rest of the year.

At the one-year mark, the full 5Cs were reassessed, and not only did psychological safety rise by 50 percent, but all 5Cs factors increased by over 20 percent in total, with these individual increases:

- Connection by 25 percent
- Candid Communication by 35 percent
- Clarity by 20 percent
- Collaboration by 20 percent
- Contribution by 10 percent

The significance of culture was underscored by Covara's financial performance, marked by a 30 percent increase in stock price over the year, completion of 100 percent of all strategic initiatives, and record-high engagement scores.

Covara's journey serves as a model for how organizations can commit to and transform their culture as a foundation for achieving results and fostering thriving communities. Emphasizing the final Contribution factor provides a pathway for organizations to reach their full potential.

Key Takeaways

Contribution drives organizational performance, directly impacts engagement and morale, and leads to a positive work environment where people feel seen, heard, and valued.

Shared vision and purpose refer to the alignment and commitment of all members toward a unified team direction. Create a shared vision that is simple and easy to remember.

Defining core values and integrating them into daily actions, discussions, and decisions creates the company's internal compass.

The greatest action organizations can take to enhance the impact subfactor is to connect people in the company to the people they impact.

Meaning and mattering refers to recognizing and valuing each individual's Contributions to the team and organization. Consider creating more opportunities to celebrate others through activities like the Prism of Praise.

Main Barriers to Overcome

Unacknowledged efforts: We don't connect daily work to a larger sense of purpose often enough. People want to know that their effort matters, that it contributes to something bigger than a to-do list. When leaders fail to connect the dots between individual roles and the broader mission, work becomes task-focused rather than mission-driven. Over time, this erodes motivation, meaning, and a sense of shared impact. To shift this, leaders must consistently translate the *what* into the *why*—helping people see how their work advances the vision and aligns with what the organization stands for.

Unlived values: We focus on crafting the right words but fall short in defining the behaviors that bring them to life. Many organizations invest heavily in articulating purpose, values, and vision, but stop at the language used to do so effectively. Without translating those words into clear, observable behaviors, people are left guessing what it actually looks like to live the values or contribute to the mission. Values don't drive action unless they are modeled, reinforced, and made real in the day-to-day.

CHAPTER 7

The Journey Ahead

Every part of the 5Cs Model is connected, because your culture is a system. Strengthen one area, and the others rise with it. That's the power of an intentional approach to leadership. The model serves as a road map for understanding what creates high-performing teams and thriving cultures. It illustrates how everything is interconnected, helping you develop your team to the highest levels and create an organizational culture you can be proud of.

Let's revisit each of the 5Cs—not just as concepts, but as practices that shape the day-to-day experience of your team and culture.

Connection

Connection reflects the level of relation everyone feels with each other. It encompasses the subfactors of trust and well-being. These two aspects enable teams and organizations to build onto every single layer of the model. Connection is the individual element most predictive of job satisfaction. High Connection is the heart of how organizations accomplish all aspects of their goals.

Candid Communication

Candid Communication is about open, straightforward, unambiguous dialogue within a team and organization. It involves psychological safety, healthy conflict and feedback, transparency, and idea meritocracy. It's about cultivating an environment where people are transparent, direct, and free from hidden agendas. Candid Communication is built on the strong core of Connection. Without both of those, we don't get the best from people. Candid Communication is the best predictor of performance out of all the factors.

Clarity

Clarity in a team and organization refers to how clear people are regarding their responsibilities, the processes they follow, and the overarching goals. A high level of Clarity helps eliminate ambiguities, ensuring that each task and decision is well-informed and purpose-driven. While this factor seems obvious, it is often not an area of focus for teams and organizations, though it is crucial for ensuring they perform at their best.

Collaboration

Collaboration is not just working in close proximity or within the same group; it involves interdependence to achieve high-level outcomes that cannot be realized individually. Collaboration requires focus, intentionality, and effort. It is essential for bringing people together in a meaningful way and for solving complex problems. For companies to reap the benefits of Collaboration, they must concentrate on three key areas: team support, accountability, and excellence.

Contribution

Contribution, the final factor in the 5Cs Model, encompasses impact, core values, meaning and mattering, and shared vision. It is the factor in which we see people get the deepest levels of fulfillment from their work. Contribution reflects how people's beliefs and actions align with the organization's core values, purpose, impact, and sense of meaning and mattering to their team and organization. It drives organizational performance, directly impacts engagement and morale, and leads to a positive work environment where people feel seen, heard, and valued.

Covara Conclusion

Lena walked into her leadership team meeting and felt something she hadn't felt in a long time: ease. The room was still full of strong opinions but shaped by trust, not tension. People asked hard questions, offered real feedback, and stayed at the table even when things got uncomfortable. They had become a team in the truest sense of the word. It hadn't been perfect. There were missteps, missed cues, and moments that tested their commitment. But the 5Cs gave them something they hadn't had before: a shared language and road map forward. Lena hadn't just learned how to lead differently. She had helped build a team and culture where people could thrive, and that had changed everything.

The Science Behind the 5Cs

I will not take pages and pages here to detail our entire research journey. However, I wanted to provide a brief summary of our work for those seeking a high-level overview of the science behind the 5Cs. All of our research, methodology, and statistics are available in a white paper if you are interested in diving deeper. You can find the link under the appendix section.

We conducted five studies to validate the structure of the 5Cs and the item set measuring it. In the first study, we used 195 items measuring the team aspect and 195 items for organizational culture, all based on our previous research and established scales. This first study helped us outline the rough framework and subfactors of the 5Cs, which we then narrowed down to 91 items. The second study was aimed at further refining the initial structure found in the first. Using the identified factor structure as a foundation for psychometric development, we were able to refine the model and items. Additionally, the second study led to the creation of agreement scores, which gauged the consistency of individuals' experiences across each factor. Studies three through five focused on continually testing potential subfactors and further refining the items. Using our dataset, we were able to streamline each scale down to 48 items and finalize the 5Cs factor and subfactor structure. We're committed to continuing our research and plan to update the model as new information emerges.

Where to Start

If you try to change everything at once, often nothing will happen. Behavioral change leading to transformation is most effective when approached step-by-step. We developed not only the model but also the tool to measure it for this very reason. Knowing where to focus first does not need to be a guessing game for your team or organization. By taking the 5Cs assessment as an initial step, you can identify where to concentrate your efforts and take action. The assessment takes an average of seven minutes and provides a clear picture of strengths, opportunities, and how consistently people feel about each factor. The quantitative data enables you to direct your efforts to the most needed area first, and since all factors are interconnected, improving one area will positively influence the others. You can find the link for the 5Cs Assessment under the appendix section.

If, for any reason, you prefer not to start with the measurement tool, I suggest navigating through the model from the inside out—beginning with Connection and its subfactors, then progressing to Candid Communication. Connection is the factor that most significantly impacts all other layers within the model.

It can be overwhelming to think about the entire journey all at once. Remember, transformations take time, focus, and intentionality. It is the constant drumbeat that leads to changing a team and an organization. As CEO, you are the drumbeat. Your presence, your priorities, and your consistency set the rhythm for culture. This is not a one-and-done off-site, a single keynote speaker, a new book to read, or even a standalone program. The journey to a cohesive, high-performing team and thriving culture takes your focus and prioritization, but not everything must be done at once.

I know that you would like to put the pedal to the metal and drive things at a fast pace. Plus, patience may not be your greatest strength. However, when it comes to human systems and moving them in the right direction, it's critical. Going too quickly, being too structured, or focusing on simply checking a box will not move the needle in the long term. Most failed culture efforts weren't poorly intentioned—they were undercommitted.

As CEO, your follow-through is the difference between a movement and a moment. The 5Cs Model is more than a framework—it's a mirror and a map. It reflects where you are, reveals where you need to go, and offers a path forward, one deliberate step at a time. It allows you to measure what matters, build what lasts, and lead with intention. This journey isn't easy, but it is meaningful. The leaders who commit to embracing the 5Cs Model create teams and cultures that perform well *and* thrive.

So as you take this work forward, I leave you with this:

- May you have the strength to lead with heart
- The courage to speak the truth with care
- The clarity to see what matters most
- The collaboration to elevate others

And the deep sense of contribution that reminds you that your leadership matters.

I wish you patience, joy, and continued commitment as you build the cohesive team and connected culture your organization deserves, while leaving a lasting legacy you can be proud of.

APPENDIX

The Principles 5Cs Assessment

The Principles 5Cs Assessment is a research-based diagnostic designed to help organizations and teams measure and improve the five core drivers of cohesive teams and thriving cultures: Connection, Candid Communication, Clarity, Collaboration, and Contribution.

What It Measures

The assessment includes 48 questions, just 3 per subfactor, and can be completed in approximately 7 minutes. It provides actionable insight across:

- 5 cultural dimensions (the 5Cs)
- 16 rigorously validated subfactors, including Trust, Psychological Safety, Healthy Conflict & Feedback, Shared Vision, and more.

The Science Behind the Tool

The Principles 5Cs Assessment is grounded in **deep academic rigor and practical relevance**. A full white paper is available if you'd like to explore the complete psychometric process (please visit https://principlesus.com/organizational-team-culture-assessment-principles-5cs-assessment/).

Rather than rely on anecdotal observations or outdated models, we built the 5Cs framework on a strong foundation of organizational psychology theory, validated measurement practices, and real-world relevance for leaders and teams. Over the course of its development, the tool has been tested and refined across tens of thousands of participants from a wide range of industries, seniority levels, and geographies.

Our research and validation process included:

- Six formal development and testing phases, spanning initial item generation, pilot studies, and psychometric refinement
- Data from diverse samples including:
  - Large-scale panels from research platforms like Prolific Academic
  - Research in a Fortune 25 company
  - Thousands of PrinciplesYou and PrinciplesUs users
- An iterative item reduction process that distilled over 195 original items to the final 48-item structure—3 items each across 16 validated subfactors
- Advanced statistical techniques, including:
  - Exploratory and confirmatory factor analysis
  - Network analysis to verify structural integrity and clustering
  - Reliability testing, with omega coefficients consistently above .85
  - Cross-sample replication to ensure generalizability

- Outcome analysis showing predictive validity for:
  - Job satisfaction
  - Supervisor- and self-rated performance
  - Perceived organizational health and ability to thrive
- Critically, the tool was shown to be distinct from personality traits, confirming it captures team and organizational culture rather than individual disposition

The result is a psychometrically rigorous and practitioner-friendly tool that captures what truly drives team cohesion and cultural health.

How It Helps

As management consultant Peter Drucker said, "You can't manage what you can't measure." Upon completion, participants receive a clear, intuitive report that highlights:

- Their scores on each of the 5Cs and the 16 subfactors
- Comparison to normalized benchmarks and outcomes
- Key insights and recommendations to enhance team cohesion, trust, communication, and alignment

Example Report

The next pages include a sample report, which demonstrates the output a team or organization would receive. This example highlights how the results are presented and interpreted to drive cultural insight and targeted action. The Principles 5Cs Assessment was built to bridge the gap between research and real-world leadership, delivering scientifically grounded insights in a format that's both accessible and actionable. By rigorously validating each component and continuously refining the tool across diverse populations, we've ensured it can serve as a reliable compass for leaders committed to building cohesive, high-performing teams and thriving cultures. Whether you're using the results to spark meaningful dialogue, identify areas for growth, or measure cultural progress over time, this assessment is designed to empower intentional leadership and measurable change.

Sample Principles 5Cs Culture Report

All Participants

251 Participants | **100%** Completion Rate

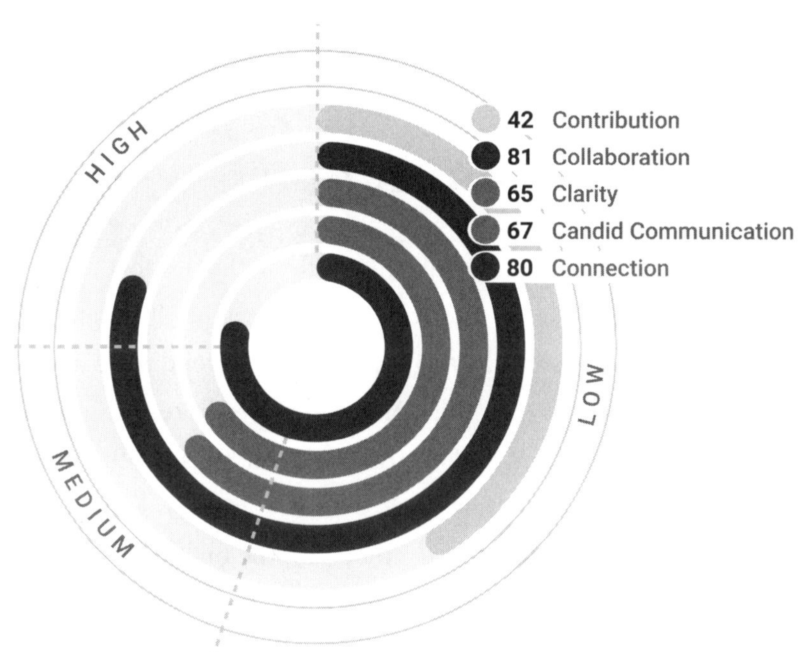

OVERVIEW

Connection is high, which indicates a high level of trust and well-being is present.

Candid Communication is moderate, signaling a need for targeted improvements to build on the existing level of transparency and open exchange of information.

Clarity is moderate, suggesting people have a solid understanding of their roles and goals, yet clearer articulation could further enhance organizational effectiveness.

Collaboration is high, reflecting a culture that is high in effective teamwork.

Contribution is low, indicating that strategies may be needed to improve the how peoples' efforts are tied to the organization's objectives.

CONNECTION

Connection within an organization reflects the ties that members feel with the entity's ethos and with their colleagues. It encapsulates a deep sense of trust and belonging that goes beyond mere association or involvement. When this bond is nurtured, it results in higher engagement, dedication, and a drive to see the organization and its people thrive.

With a high score of 80 in Connection, the organization stands out for its ability to foster strong interpersonal bonds among its members. The atmosphere is characterized by a deep sense of unity, mutual trust, and a shared sense of purpose. Employees feel a genuine bond with their peers, which not only bolsters team dynamics but also contributes to an inclusive and harmonious workplace environment.

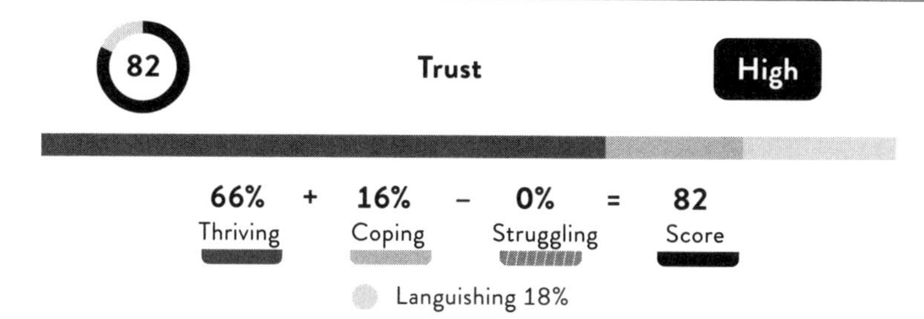

Trust refers to the trustworthiness and mutual trust that is fostered and reflected within the organization. A high score of 82 for Trust signifies a robust foundation of mutual confidence among employees within the organization. Trustworthiness isn't just an aspirational trait but is widely recognized and manifested in actions. The bedrock of this positive score lies in the shared belief in the intentions of colleagues and the broader organizational ethos. In such an environment, employees are more inclined to collaborate, take initiatives, and believe in the shared vision of the organization.

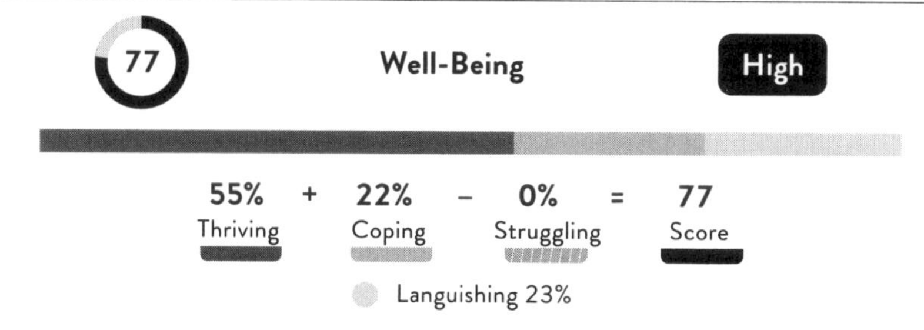

Well-Being is a measure of the emphasis placed on physical, mental, and emotional health by the organization. A high score of 77 for Well-Being indicates that the organization excels in prioritizing the holistic well-being of its employees. Physical, mental, and emotional health are consistently acknowledged and nurtured. In such a supportive environment, employees feel they can genuinely focus on self-care and achieve a balanced work-life dynamic. This high score underscores the organization's commitment to fostering an environment where well-being is not just spoken about but genuinely practiced.

CANDID COMMUNICATION

Candid Communication champions the principle of straightforward, unambiguous discourse within the organization. It's about cultivating an environment where dialogue is transparent, direct, and free from hidden agendas. This openness enriches information flow, ensuring that feedback and discussions are genuine, leading to an atmosphere where trust is both extended and received.

A moderate score of 67 for Candid Communication suggests a balanced atmosphere where communication is generally open, but there could be instances or areas where information is not as transparently shared as it could be. The organization might benefit from promoting further openness and ensuring that all members feel at ease to share insights, concerns, and feedback without hesitation.

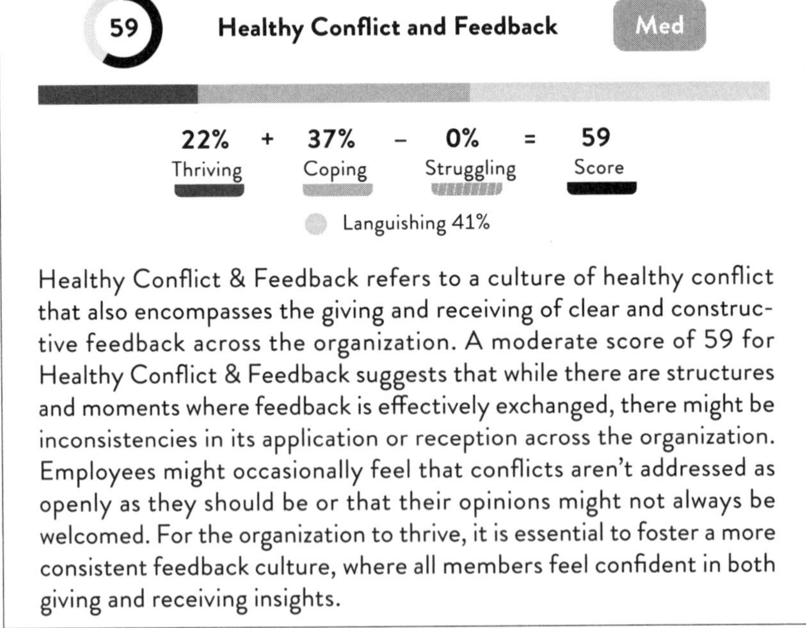

Healthy Conflict & Feedback refers to a culture of healthy conflict that also encompasses the giving and receiving of clear and constructive feedback across the organization. A moderate score of 59 for Healthy Conflict & Feedback suggests that while there are structures and moments where feedback is effectively exchanged, there might be inconsistencies in its application or reception across the organization. Employees might occasionally feel that conflicts aren't addressed as openly as they should be or that their opinions might not always be welcomed. For the organization to thrive, it is essential to foster a more consistent feedback culture, where all members feel confident in both giving and receiving insights.

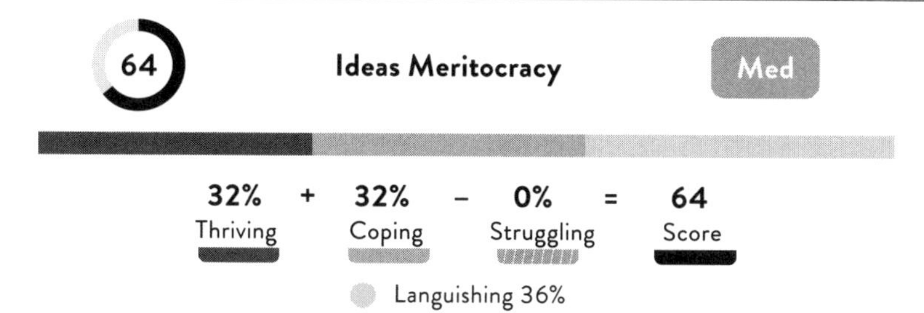

Ideas Meritocracy refers to the degree to which the organization values and rewards the best ideas, regardless of their source. A moderate score of 64 for Ideas Meritocracy suggests the organization appreciates the value of diverse contributions and strives to judge them on their merits. However, there may be instances where hierarchy or status unduly influences the consideration of ideas. While there is a foundation for a merit-based culture, there is a need for more consistent application of this principle. Developing clearer guidelines for evaluating ideas and creating more platforms for unbiased idea sharing could enhance the meritocratic nature of the organization, ensuring that all voices have equal opportunity to be heard.

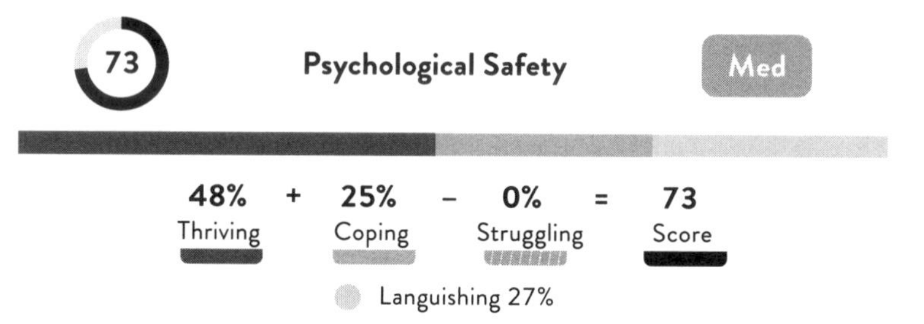

Psychological Safety refers to the degree to which employees feel safe to express concerns, vulnerabilities, and dissenting views without fear. A moderate score of 73 for Psychological Safety suggests that while there are instances where employees feel safe to voice concerns and be vulnerable, there are moments or areas where this sense of security might waver. This mixed perception can sometimes limit open communication and the free exchange of ideas. Strengthening the organizational structures and channels that promote psychological safety can further enhance the sense of trust and openness among employees.

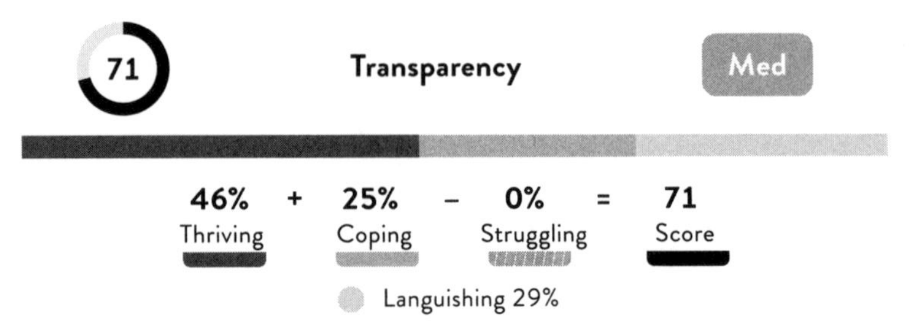

Transparency within an organization relates to the openness and accessibility of information and decision-making processes to all members. A moderate score of 71 for Transparency suggests that while the organization values openness and honesty, there might be room for further consistency in its application. The principles of radical honesty and transparent communication are recognized, but there may be instances where information flow isn't as seamless as desired. Enhancing channels for open communication and reinforcing the importance of transparency can boost trust and alignment within the organization.

CLARITY

Clarity in an organization refers to the distinctness of its mission, vision, objectives, and operational processes. A high level of Clarity ensures that every member has a transparent understanding of their roles, the organization's overarching goals, and the path to achieve them. This lucidity is vital for eliminating ambiguities, ensuring that each task and decision is well informed and purpose driven.

A moderate score of 65 in Clarity indicates that, while many members have a fair understanding of their roles and the organization's direction, there might be some areas of ambiguity or misalignment. It would be beneficial for the organization to refine communication channels, offer clearer guidelines, and ensure that every team member understands their individual role and how it aligns with the organization's objectives.

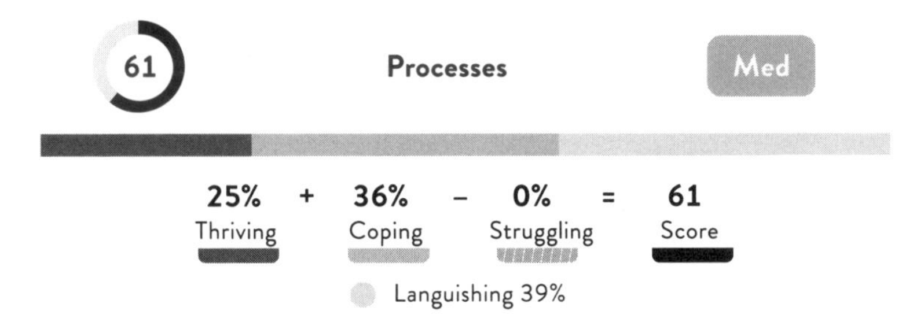

Processes refers to the clarity and documentation of operational workflows and systems used by the organization. A moderate score of 61 for Processes points to some gaps in the thoroughness or communication of operational methodologies. While some aspects of the organization's operations may be well-defined and streamlined, there might be areas where processes aren't as clear or systems aren't effectively utilized. Addressing these gaps will not only enhance operational efficiency but also provide employees with clearer direction, reducing potential friction points.

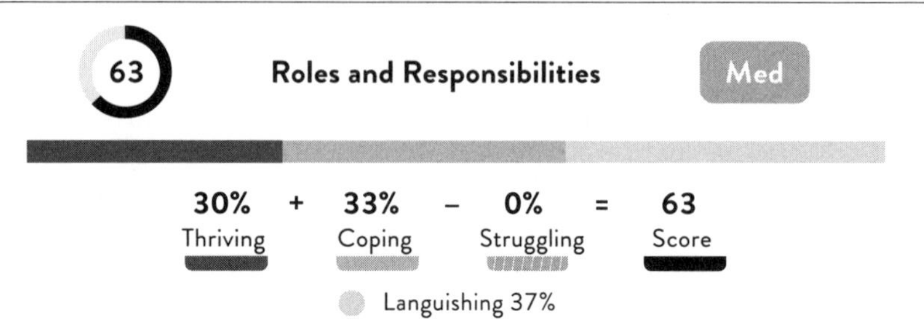

Roles & Responsibilities refers to the clarity and definition provided around individual tasks, authority, and expectations within the organization. A moderate score of 63 for Roles & Responsibilities suggests some inconsistencies in the clear definition and communication of roles within the organization. While some employees may feel confident in their tasks and authority, others might occasionally encounter ambiguity or overlaps in responsibilities. Addressing these areas of uncertainty may be needed to ensure efficiency, prevent potential misunderstandings, and allow employees to fully invest in their roles with clarity and confidence.

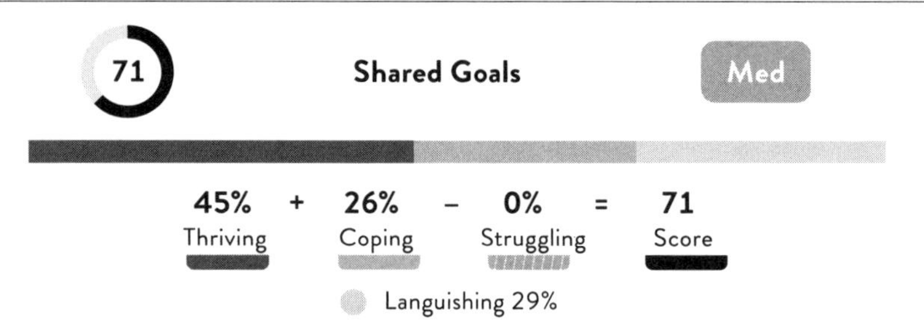

Shared Goals refers to the alignment and clarity of organizational priorities, goals, and the resources allocated to achieve them. A moderate score of 71 for Shared Goals suggests that while there is some alignment between organizational priorities and goals, there might be room for improvement in the communication or realization of these priorities. This might lead to occasions where employees might not be entirely clear on the top objectives or how resources are being allocated. Enhancing clarity around these aspects can support better alignment and more effective direction for the entire team.

COLLABORATION

Collaboration emphasizes members working in concert to achieve common goals and foster performance excellence. It involves blending diverse skills and perspectives while maintaining individual accountability. In a collaborative environment, combined knowledge is harnessed, often leading to solutions that are both innovative and effective, transcending what individuals could achieve in isolation.

With a high score of 81 for Collaboration, the organization excels in fostering a cooperative and synergetic environment. Members work cohesively, share knowledge, and support one another in achieving shared objectives. This positive collaborative atmosphere boosts team productivity and ensures that collective efforts yield fruitful results.

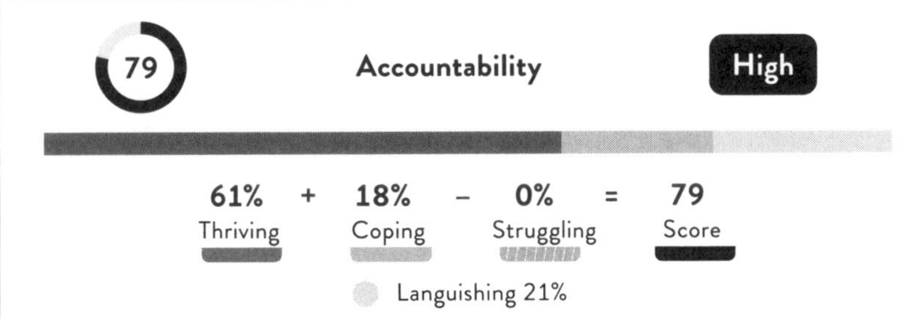

Accountability measures the commitment to holding individuals and groups within the organization responsible for their performance in a fair and consistent manner. A high score of 79 for Accountability reflects a strong emphasis on individual responsibility within the organization. This culture ensures that every team member is held accountable for the organization's overall performance. Moreover, when commitments aren't met, there's a collaborative effort to address and rectify the situation. Such consistent and rigorous accountability standards, applicable to everyone, paired with strict checks and balances for decisions, foster a transparent and responsible working environment.

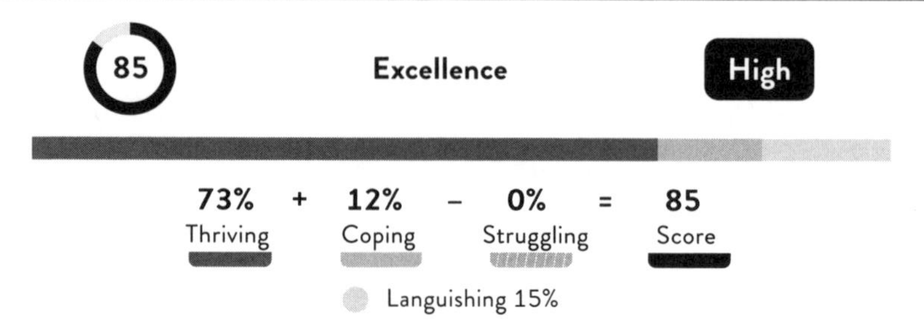

Excellence refers to the drive towards high performance, the rejection of mediocrity, and the desire to learn from mistakes. A high score of 85 for Excellence suggests that the organization places a strong emphasis on continuous improvement and achieving superior performance. In this environment, merely being average isn't considered satisfactory. There's a clear expectation that every individual should learn from their mistakes. Furthermore, the focus is squarely on actual performance rather than just commendations or verbal appreciation. Such an environment fosters growth and drives employees to consistently elevate their standards and outcomes.

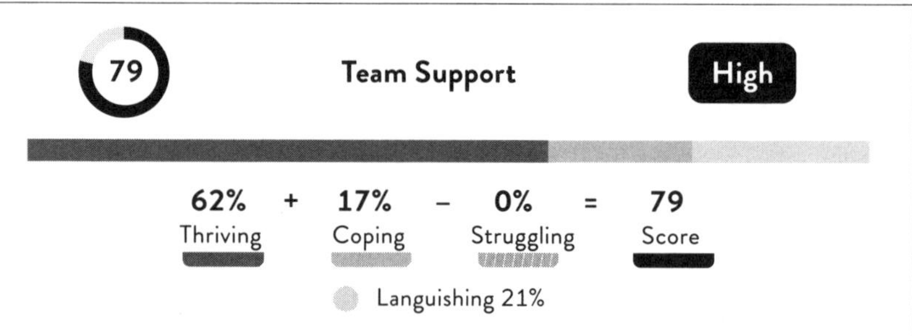

Team Support refers to the willingness and consistency of employees to go beyond their roles to aid and support their colleagues. A high score of 79 for Team Support underscores a thriving culture where employees are proactive in assisting one another. Not only do team members regularly step in to aid their colleagues, but they also provide essential support during challenging and stressful times. Such a cohesive environment indicates a profound sense of camaraderie and mutual respect, fostering a supportive workplace where individuals feel valued and cared for by their peers.

CONTRIBUTION

Contribution reflects how team actions align with the organization's core values and goals. Every member's role is meaningful to them and essential in driving company success and resonating with stakeholders. It emphasizes recognizing each member's efforts and their broader impact, ensuring that work benefits both the organization and its customers.

A low score of 42 in Contribution signifies that there's a perceived gap in recognizing individual efforts and their alignment with organizational and stakeholder goals. Enhancing feedback mechanisms, aligning individual roles with broader objectives, and consistently acknowledging efforts can aid in bridging this gap and ensuring everyone feels their Contributions are meaningful.

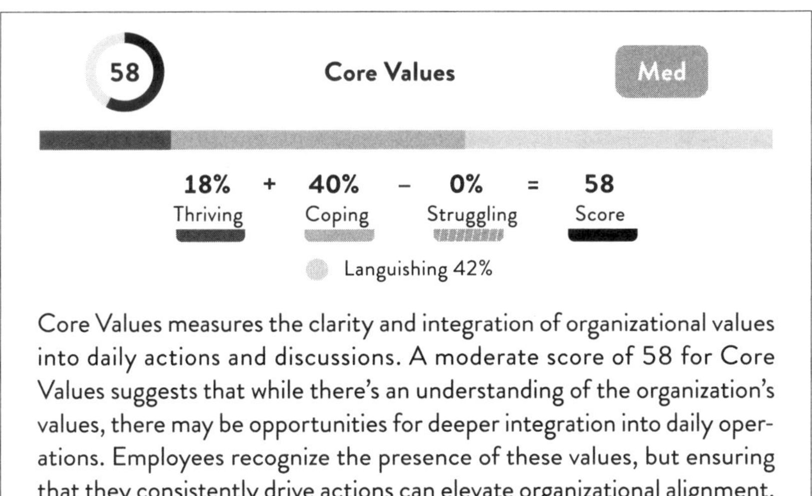

Core Values measures the clarity and integration of organizational values into daily actions and discussions. A moderate score of 58 for Core Values suggests that while there's an understanding of the organization's values, there may be opportunities for deeper integration into daily operations. Employees recognize the presence of these values, but ensuring that they consistently drive actions can elevate organizational alignment. Strengthening this connection can lead to more meaningful discussions and decisions that truly resonate with the organization's ethos.

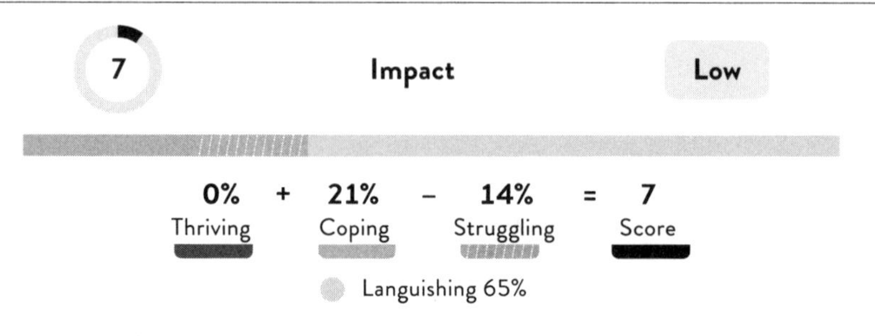

Impact refers to the emphasis on generating meaningful outcomes that benefit stakeholders and the broader community. A low score of 7 for Impact indicates that there's considerable scope for the organization to amplify its focus on delivering meaningful outcomes. While there might be some appreciation for teams' efforts, there's a need to ensure that these endeavors consistently translate into tangible benefits for stakeholders. Elevating this focus can enhance the organization's influence and ensure it consistently creates value for its customers and stakeholders alike.

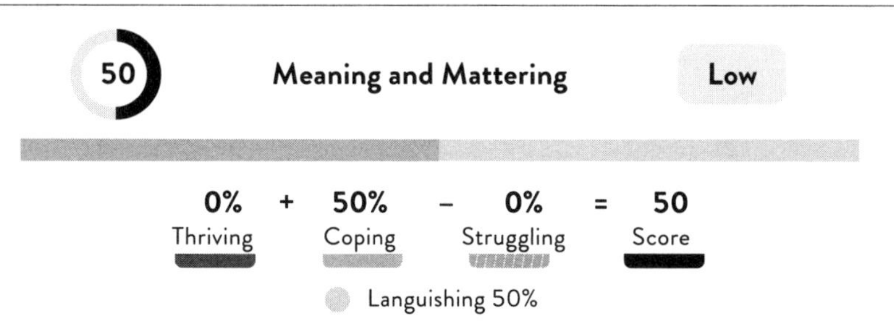

Meaning & Mattering refers to the recognition and sense of value of each individual's contribution to the organization. A low score of 50 for Meaning & Mattering suggests that there's an opportunity for the organization to strengthen its recognition and appreciation efforts. Employees might not consistently feel that their contributions are acknowledged or that they hold value within the organizational framework. Enhancing acknowledgment mechanisms and emphasizing the importance of every individual's role can elevate employee engagement and promote a culture of inclusivity.

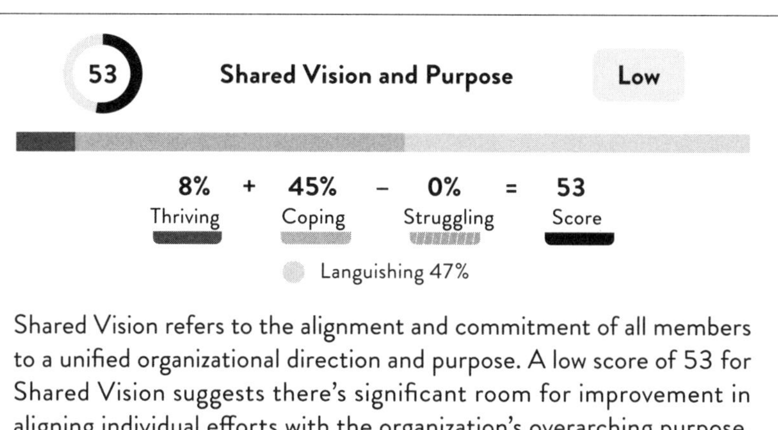

Shared Vision refers to the alignment and commitment of all members to a unified organizational direction and purpose. A low score of 53 for Shared Vision suggests there's significant room for improvement in aligning individual efforts with the organization's overarching purpose. Employees may not feel consistently connected to the shared vision, leading to potential disparities in direction and objectives. Focused initiatives to communicate, reinforce, and involve employees in the visioning process can bridge this gap, fostering greater alignment and unity.

Acknowledgments

I am proud to share that developing the 5Cs Model and assessment tool has been one of the most rewarding collaborations of my life. We lived the model even as we created it. I am truly grateful to the amazing partners involved in the research and technology behind the tool, especially those named below.

The Principles Team

As I shared earlier, meeting the Principles team was a transformational moment for my company, Connected EC, and me. I had been looking for a personality assessment tool like theirs for far too long. The rigor of the work immediately resonated with me as a researcher and with my lived experience as a coach. It has been a profound honor and a true privilege to collaborate with Ray Dalio, whose commitment to truth, principles, culture, and rigorous thinking has meaningfully shaped me as both a leader and a coach.

Collaborating with the Principles CEO, Zack Wieder, and the Head of Marketing and Strategy, Patrick Reilly, was seamless. Our mission to create cohesive, high-performing teams and thriving cultures while bridging the gap between research and practice was aligned. Zack is one of the fastest, brightest thinkers I have had the opportunity to work with. His passion and drive for helping companies are inspiring to watch. He is the kind of leader who always says what he means, is willing to ideate at a racecar pace, and is one of the most genuine people I know. Patrick is the definition of positive leadership. Every interaction I have with him leaves me with more energy and a smile on my face. His level of accountability and care for others is unwavering. Throughout my collaboration with Principles, I couldn't imagine a better team to work on the 5Cs. Not only were our company values and mission aligned, the entire team was as extraordinary as Zack and Patrick.

Leader and Organization Vitality Center

I am fortunate to work with amazing organizational psychologists in our Leader and Organization Vitality (LOV) Center, particularly Beggi Olafs, a brilliant PhD and coach who was instrumental in helping us with the 5Cs project. Beggi reviewed over 100 papers on teams and organizational performance to create a starting point for the 5Cs that incorporated the most current research and science.

To Those Who Lit the Way

Throughout my life, I've been fortunate to cross paths with some of the most extraordinary people—in work, in friendship, and in all the spaces in between. While I wish I could name every person who has shaped my path, lifted me up, or helped me grow, it would take a book of its own. To all who have inspired, supported, and walked beside me, thank you from the bottom of my heart.

Sarah, your humility, grounded presence, and willingness to lead as your full, authentic self create a space where creativity, possibility, and trust flourish. You made it not only possible, but safe, for me to share a bold idea in its earliest, roughest form, and your immediate partnership and unwavering support helped bring the 5Cs to life. Karen, your belief in me, your joy, and the trust and leadership you extended to our team made even the most ambitious vision feel possible. You are a constant positive light to everyone around you, illuminating people's strengths and lifting those in your presence.

Ken, your dedication to people, culture, and team has left a profound mark on me. The way you foster trust and build uplifting environments makes it a true joy to be in your orbit. Mostafa, you are one of the most caring and authentic leaders I've ever known. Your energy lights up every room, and your leadership leaves a lasting imprint. Helen, you were on my heart with every word I wrote. Your clarity, courage, and deep compassion embody what it means to lead with both strength and heart. You lead with grace and conviction. Pablo, thank you for your steady presence, thoughtful insight, and generous spirit. Your leadership has shaped my thinking meaningfully. Kellyn, your leadership shines brightly through your unwavering passion for people and culture, transforming the world around you. Thank you for believing in me and in this work.

Steve, you've been my greatest champion from the very beginning. Thank you for taking a chance on me, for always having my back, and for never wavering in your belief. Larry, thank you for making this world a better place through your vision and leadership. I am constantly learning from you and grateful for our connection. Julie, you are an extraordinary leader with a deep and unwavering commitment to people and culture. Your support of me and this work has meant more than you know, and your friendship is one I deeply value. Paul, your wisdom and perspective have opened doors in both thought and action. Thank you for always seeing what's possible. Dave, your support has helped me grow in ways I never imagined. Thank you for being a powerful example of what it means to lead with purpose, presence, and integrity.

Stewart, thank you for guiding me in bridging the gap between research and practice. Your guidance, support, and partnership have truly changed my life. Michelle, thank you for lighting my flame and believing in my work. You taught me how to research with rigor and heart, and your encouragement gave me the courage to share it with the world. Lindsay, your love, friendship, and leadership are a grounding force in my life. Our connection brings joy to everything we do together. Chad, you believed in me from the very beginning and helped bring Connected EC to life, seeing possibility even when I couldn't fully see it myself. Your wisdom has been a steady guide, and your friendship has meant more to me than I can put into words.

The Connected EC (CEC) Team

To the extraordinary CEC Team—in my eyes, the most impressive coaches and team on the planet—thank you. Your brilliance, love, and commitment to growth inspire me daily. This book would not exist without your support, deep wisdom, and the way you show up for others with so much courage and care. You each have played a vital role in shaping this journey, and I am endlessly grateful to be in it with you. It's an honor to work alongside you, learn from you, and build something meaningful together. Lynzi, words can't begin to express how much I appreciate all that you do for me and the team every single day. You are a gift!

5Cs Book Team

To the entire team at Ideapress, thank you for your care, professionalism, and belief in this work. Your partnership, dedication, and steady guidance helped bring this book into the world, and I am deeply grateful to each of you. Thank you for seeing this book's potential and for holding my hand through the entire process. Catherine, your guidance, wisdom, and coaching have supported me through so many pivotal moments in my path. Thank you for your care, your insight, and your friendship. Trudi, I can't thank you enough for making this book come to life. Your editing expertise was the catalyst that shaped this book into what it is today. Rachael, thank you for always seeing more in me than I see in myself; your support throughout this process has been transformational. Jen, I'm not sure how I got so lucky to have you by my side for this journey. Your insight, strategy, and leadership have made all the difference, and I truly could not do this without you.

My Loving Family

Thank you for being the steady, loving foundation beneath everything I do. Sam, my incredible husband, your belief in me has never wavered. Your love, partnership, and quiet strength continue to be my anchor and my home. You remind me every day what it means to be truly seen and supported. I could not have written this, nor become the woman I am, without you by my side.

Jack and Ella, you are my heart. You inspire me with your courage, curiosity, and deep empathy for the world around you. You remind me every day what matters most. Thank you for giving me the time and space to bring this book to life, and for being the brightest lights in mine.

Dad, your wisdom, strength, and unconditional love continue to guide me. I carry your lessons with me always. Mom, your love remains my North Star. Thank you for teaching me that real leadership begins with kindness, patience, and generosity of spirit. To my brother, Scott, your steady presence, wise perspective, and constant belief in me mean more than words can express. I'm endlessly grateful for our bond and your presence in my life. And to my extended family, you've held me, lifted me, and loved me through every season. I am so lucky to walk through life with all of you in my corner.

About the Author

Jamie Shapiro is a CEO coach, organizational psychologist, and the bestselling author of *Brilliant: Be the Leader Who Shines Brightly Without Burning Out*. She is the founder and CEO of Connected EC, a leadership coaching firm known for its team-based, whole-person approach to developing executives and transforming culture. She is a Master Certified Executive Coach, professional speaker, researcher, expert facilitator, and certified nutritionist. She holds a PhD in Positive Organizational Psychology, an MBA, and a Master of Science in Information Technology, academic foundations that complement her real-world leadership experience and research-driven approach. Jamie brings a unique and deeply integrated lens to leadership, combining evidence-based insights with practical, real-world application.

Jamie has been coaching and developing high-performing teams since 1998 in executive roles within large-scale corporate companies and now externally. She left the corporate world with a mission: to change the way leaders show up for themselves, their teams, and their organizations. She specializes in supporting CEOs and their executive teams through growth, complexity, and cultural transformation.

Jamie is also the founder of the Leader and Organization Vitality (LOV) Center, a research institute dedicated to unlocking cutting-edge research to build thriving organizational cultures. Through the LOV Center, she helps bridge the gap between science and practice, ensuring leaders have access to the latest insights on leadership, vitality, performance, and culture.

She lives in Longmont, Colorado, with her loving husband, Sam, and two incredible teenagers, Jack and Ella, who remind her every day of what matters most. The family dogs, Diesel and Luna, help to ensure the house is always filled with energy and affection.

Endnotes

1 Keller, Scott, Mary Meany, and Caroline Pung. "Losing from Day One: Why Even Successful Transformations Fall Short." McKinsey & Company. December 7, 2021. https://www.mckinsey.com/capabilities/people-and-organizational-performance/our-insights/successful-transformations.

2 Center for Creative Leadership. "Are You Getting the Best out of Your Senior Leadership Team?" March 31, 2020. https://www.ccl.org/articles/white-papers/getting-best-executive-team/.

3 Dale Carnegie. "A Leadership Imperative: Creating a Culture of High-Performing Teams." 2023. https://www.dalecarnegie.com/en/resources/a-leadership-imperative-creating-a-culture-of-high-performing-teams.

4 Drucker, Peter F. *The Practice of Management.* Harper & Row, 1954.

5 Harter, Jim. "US Employee Engagement Inches Up Slightly After 11-Year Low." Gallup. July 25, 2024. https://www.gallup.com/workplace/647564/employee-engagement-inches-slightly-year-low.aspx.

6 Robinson, Harry. "Why Do Most Transformations Fail? A Conversation with Harry Robinson." McKinsey & Company. July 10, 2019. https://www.mckinsey.com/capabilities/transformation/our-insights/why-do-most-transformations-fail-a-conversation-with-harry-robinson.

7 Keller, Scott. "High-Performing Teams: A Timeless Leadership Topic." McKinsey & Company. June 28, 2017. https://www.mckinsey.com/capabilities/people-and-organizational-performance/our-insights/high-performing-teams-a-timeless-leadership-topic.

8 Bailinson, Peter, William Decherd, Diana Ellsworth, and Maital Guttman. "Understanding Organizational Barriers to a More Inclusive Workplace." McKinsey & Company. June 23, 2020. https://www.mckinsey.com/capabilities/people-and-organizational-performance/our-insights/understanding-organizational-barriers-to-a-more-inclusive-workplace.

9 Buczynska, Ela, Tom Handcock, and Gabrielle Lieberman. "How CEOs Can Build and Maintain a High-Performing C-suite." Russell Reynolds. December 4, 2023. https://www.russellreynolds.com/en/insights/articles/how-ceos-can-build-and-maintain-a-high-performing-csuite.

10 Society for Human Resource Management. "SHRM Reports Toxic Workplace Cultures Cost Billions." September 25, 2019. https://www.shrm.org/about/press-room/shrm-reports-toxic-workplace-cultures-cost-billions.

11 Eagle Hill Consulting. "Corporate Culture and the C-Suite Agenda: Culture Is Critical, but Undervalued by the C-Suite." 2019. https://www.eaglehillconsulting.com/wp-content/uploads/EHC-Opinion-Culture-Valuation-Survey.pdf.

12 Kotter, John P. and James L. Heskett. *Corporate Culture and Performance.* Simon and Schuster, 2008.

13 Kitterman, Ted. "When Employees Thrive, Companies More Than Triple Their Stock Market Performance." Great Place to Work. April 2, 2025. https://www.greatplacetowork.com/resources/blog/when-employees-thrive-companies-triple-their-stock-market-performance.

14 Patel, Alok and Stephanie Plowman. "The Increasing Importance of a Best Friend at Work." Gallup. Last modified January 19, 2024. https://www.gallup.com/workplace/397058/increasing-importance-best-friend-work.aspx.

15 Hedrick, Katelyn, Ben Wigert, and Ryan Pendell. "Despite Employer Prioritization, Employee Wellbeing Falters." Gallup. November 3, 2024. https://www.gallup.com/workplace/652769/despite-employer-prioritization-employee-wellbeing-falters.aspx.

16 Zak, Paul J. "The Neuroscience of Trust." *Harvard Business Review*, January–February 2017. https://hbr.org/2017/01/the-neuroscience-of-trust.

17 Deci, Edward L. and Richard M. Ryan. "Self-Determination Theory." *Handbook of Theories of Social Psychology 1*, no. 20 (2012): 416–436. https://doi.org/10.4135/9781446249215.n21.

18 Breuer, Christina, Joachim Hüffmeier, and Guido Hertel. "Does Trust Matter More in Virtual Teams? A Meta-Analysis of Trust and Team Effectiveness Considering Virtuality and Documentation as Moderators." *Journal of Applied Psychology* 101, no. 8 (2016): 1151–1177. https://doi.org/10.1037/apl0000113.

19 Trusted Advisor Associates LLC. "The Trust Equation." Accessed September 30, 2025. https://trustedadvisor.com/why-trust-matters/understanding-trust/understanding-the-trust-equation.

20 Brown, Brené. *Dare to Lead: Brave Work. Tough Conversations. Whole Hearts.* Random House, 2018.

21 Brown, Brené. *Daring Greatly: How the Courage to Be Vulnerable Transforms the Way We Live, Love, Parent, and Lead.* Gotham Books, 2012.

22 De Jong, Bart A., Kurt T. Dirks, and Nicole Gillespie. "Trust and Team Performance: A Meta-Analysis of Main Effects, Moderators, and Covariates." *Journal of Applied Psychology* 101, no. 8 (2016): 1134–1150. https://doi.org/10.1037/apl0000110.

23 Dirks, Kurt T. and Donald L. Ferrin. "The Role of Trust in Organizational Settings." *Organization Science* 12, no. 4 (2001): 450–467. https://doi.org/10.1287/orsc.12.4.450.10640.

24 Kouzes, James M. and Barry Z. Posner. *The Leadership Challenge: How to Make Extraordinary Things Happen in Organizations.* 7th ed. Jossey-Bass, 2023.

25 Zhao, Minxiang, Yixuan Li, Junqi Lin, et al. "The Relationship Between Trust and Well-Being: A Meta-Analysis." *Journal of Happiness Studies* 25, no. 56 (2024):1–26. https://doi.org/10.1007/s10902-024-00737-8.

26 Zak, Paul J. "The Neuroscience of Trust." *Harvard Business Review*, January–February 2017. https://hbr.org/2017/01/the-neuroscience-of-trust.

27 Brown, Brené. *Daring Greatly: How the Courage to Be Vulnerable Transforms the Way We Live, Love, Parent, and Lead.* Gotham Books, 2012.

28 Shapiro, Jamie. "Burning Bright or Burning Out: A Qualitative Investigation of Leader Vitality." *Frontiers in Psychology* 14 (2023). https://doi.org/10.3389/fpsyg.2023.1244089.

29 Ibid.

30 Fisher, Jen, Sue Cantrell, Jay Bhatt, and Paul Silvergate. "The Important Role of Leaders in Advancing Human Sustainability." Deloitte Insights. June 18, 2024. https://www2.deloitte.com/us/en/insights/topics/talent/workplace-well-being-research-2024.html.

31 Gallup. "State of the Global Workplace: Understanding Employees, Informing Leaders." 2025. https://www.gallup.com/workplace/349484/state-of-the-global-workplace.aspx.

32 Hannah, Sean T., Bruce J. Avolio, and Fred O. Walumbwa. "Relationships Between Authentic Leadership, Moral Courage, and Ethical and Pro-Social Behaviors." *Business Ethics Quarterly* 21, no. 4 (2011): 555–578. https://doi.org/10.5840/beq201121436.

33 Detert, James R. and Amy C. Edmondson. "Why Employees Are Afraid to Speak." *Harvard Business Review*, May 2007. https://hbr.org/2007/05/why-employees-are-afraid-to-speak.

34 Detert, Jim and Evan Bruno. "The Courage to Be Candid." *MIT Sloan Management Review*, June 1, 2021. https://sloanreview.mit.edu/article/the-courage-to-be-candid/.

35 Edmondson, Amy C. *The Fearless Organization: Creating Psychological Safety in the Workplace for Learning, Innovation, and Growth.* Wiley, 2018.

Carroll, John S. and Amy C. Edmondson. "Leading Organisational Learning in Health Care." *BMJ Quality & Safety* 11, no. 1 (2002): 51–56. https://doi.org/10.1136/qhc.11.1.51.

Edmondson, Amy. "Psychological Safety and Learning Behavior in Work Teams." *Administrative Science Quarterly* 44, no. 2 (1999): 350–383. https://doi.org/10.2307/2666999.

36 Duhigg, Charles. "What Google Learned from Its Quest to Build the Perfect Team." *The New York Times Magazine*, February 25, 2016. https://www.nytimes.com/2016/02/28/magazine/what-google-learned-from-its-quest-to-build-the-perfect-team.html.

37 Treisman, Anne M. "Strategies and Models of Selective Attention." *Psychological Review* 76, no. 3 (1969): 282–299. https://doi.org/10.1037/h0027242.

38 Mack, Arien and Irvin Rock. *Inattentional Blindness.* The MIT Press, 1998.

39 Dalio, Ray. *Principles: Life and Work.* Simon and Schuster, 2018.

40 Frazier, M. Lance, Stav Fainshmidt, Ryan L. Klinger, et al. "Psychological Safety: A Meta-Analytic Review and Extension." *Personnel Psychology* 70, no. 1 (2016): 113–165. https://doi.org/10.1111/peps.12183.

41 Narasimhan, Vas. "How to Cultivate Psychological Safety, and Why It Matters." LinkedIn, August 4, 2021. https://www.linkedin.com/pulse/how-cultivate-psychological-safety-why-matters-test-vas-narasimhan/.

42 Larson, Erik. "Research Shows Diversity + Inclusion = Better Decision Making at Work." Cloverpop. September 25, 2017. https://www.cloverpop.com/blog/research-shows-diversity-inclusion-better-decision-making-at-work.

43 De Dreu, Carsten K. W. and Laurie R. Weingart. "Task Versus Relationship Conflict, Team Performance, and Team Member Satisfaction: A Meta-Analysis." *Journal of Applied Psychology* 88, no. 4 (2003): 741–9. https://doi.org/10.1037/0021-9010.88.4.741.

44 Grant, Adam. *Think Again: The Power of Knowing What You Don't Know.* Penguin, 2023.

45 Fredrickson, Barbara L. "The Broaden-and-Build Theory of Positive Emotions." *Philosophical Transactions of the Royal Society of London. Series B: Biological Sciences* 359, no. 1449 (2004): 1367–1377. https://doi.org/10.1098/rstb.2004.1512.

46 Roos, Carla Anne, Tom Postmes, and Namkje Koudenburg. "Feeling Heard: Operationalizing a Key Concept for Social Relations." *PLoS ONE* 18, no. 11 (2023). https://doi.org/10.1371/journal.pone.0292865.

47 Dalio, Ray. *Principles: Life and Work.* Simon and Schuster, 2018.

48 Berridge, Peter and Jen Ostrich. *Feedback Reimagined: Transform Your Organization Through Positive Psychology and Social Support.* Modern Wisdom Press, 2023.

49 Wigert, Ben and Nate Dvorak. "Feedback Is Not Enough." Gallup. May 16, 2019. https://www.gallup.com/workplace/257582/feedback-not-enough.aspx.

50 Dyer, Wayne W. *Change Your Thoughts, Change Your Life: Living the Wisdom of the Tao.* Hay House, 2009.

51 Schneider, Sandra L. "In Search of Realistic Optimism." *American Psychologist* 56, no. 3 (2001): 250–263. https://doi.org/10.1037/0003-066X.56.3.250.

52 Kleiner, Art, Peter M. Senge, Richard Ross, et al. "The Ladder of Inference." In *The Fifth Discipline Fieldbook: Strategies and Tools for Building a Learning Organization*, 242–246. Cown Currency, 1994.

53 Deloitte. 2024. "2024 Global Human Capital Trends." Deloitte Insights. https://www2.deloitte.com/content/dam/insights/articles/glob176836_global-human-capital-trends-2024/DI_Global-Human-Capital-Trends-2024.pdf.

54 Dalio, Ray. *Principles: Life and Work.* Simon and Schuster, 2018.

55 Saleem, Sharjeel, Mariam Ayub, Muhammad Mustafa Raziq, and Muhammad Zahid Iqbal. "A Multilevel Study of Authentic Leadership, Collective Efficacy, and Team Performance and Commitment." *Current Psychology* 42 (2023): 18473–18487. https://doi.org/10.1007/s12144-022-04029-3.

56 Hess, Edward D. "The Power of an Idea Meritocracy." UVA Darden Ideas to Action. April 26, 2018. https://ideas.darden.virginia.edu/the-power-of-an-idea-meritocracy.

57 Dalio, Ray. *Principles: Life and Work.* Simon and Schuster, 2018.

58 Hu, Jia and Robert C. Liden. "Antecedents of Team Potency and Team Effectiveness: An Examination of Goal and Process Clarity and Servant Leadership." *Journal of Applied Psychology* 96, no. 4 (2011): 851–862. https://doi.org/10.1037/a0022465.

Kundu, Subhash C., Sandeep Kumar, and Kusum Lata. "Effects of Perceived Role Clarity on Innovative Work Behavior: A Multiple Mediation Model." *RAUSP Management Journal* 55, no. 4 (2020): 457–472. https://doi.org/10.1108/RAUSP-04-2019-0056.

Lang, Jessica, Jeffrey L. Thomas, Paul D. Bliese, and Amy B. Adler. "Job Demands and Job Performance: The Mediating Effect of Psychological and Physical Strain and the Moderating Effect of Role Clarity." *Journal of Occupational Health Psychology* 12, no. 2 (2007): 116–124. https://doi.org/10.1037/1076-8998.12.2.116.

Van der Hoek, Marieke, Sandra Groeneveld, and Ben Kuipers. "Goal Setting in Teams: Goal Clarity and Team Performance in the Public Sector." *Review of Public Personnel Administration* 38, no. 4 (2018): 472–493. https://doi.org/10.1177/0734371X16682815.

59 Bazigos, Michael, Aaron De Smet, and Chris Gagnon. "Why Agility Pays." *McKinsey Quarterly.* December 1, 2015. https://www.mckinsey.com/capabilities/people-and-organizational-performance/our-insights/why-agility-pays.

60 Kundu, Subhash C., Sandeep Kumar, and Kusum Lata. "Effects of Perceived Role Clarity on Innovative Work Behavior: A Multiple Mediation Model." *RAUSP Management Journal* 55, no. 4 (2020): 457–472. https://doi.org/10.1108/RAUSP-04-2019-0056.

61 Project Management Institute. *A Guide to the Project Management Body of Knowledge: PMBOK® Guide.* 6th ed. Project Management Institute, Inc., 2017. https://trainupinstitute.com/wp-content/uploads/2022/03/Project-Management-Institute-A-Guide-to-the-Project-Management-Body-of-Knowledge-PMBOK®-Guide–Sixth-Edition-Project-Management-Institute-2017.pdf.

62 Hu, Jia and Robert C. Liden. "Antecedents of Team Potency and Team Effectiveness: An Examination of Goal and Process Clarity and Servant

Leadership." *Journal of Applied Psychology* 96, no. 4 (2011): 851–862. https://doi.org/10.1037/a0022465.

63 Locke, Edwin A. and Gary P. Latham. "The Development of Goal Setting Theory: A Half Century Retrospective." *Motivation Science* 5, no. 2 (2019): 93–105. https://doi.org/10.1037/mot0000127.

64 FranklinCovey. "Big Rocks." YouTube video, 4:01. August 24, 2017. https://youtu.be/zV3gMTOEWt8.

65 Covey, Stephen R. *The 7 Habits of Highly Effective People: Powerful Lessons in Personal Change.* Free Press, 1989.

66 Dyer, Wayne W. *You Are What You Think: 365 Meditations for Extraordinary Living.* Hay House, 2018.

67 Gratton, Lynda and Tamara J. Erickson. "Eight Ways to Build Collaborative Teams." *Harvard Business Review*, November 2007. https://hbr.org/2007/11/eight-ways-to-build-collaborative-teams.

68 Muir, William Martin. "Group Selection for Adaptation to Multiple-Hen Cages: Selection Program and Direct Responses." *Poultry Science* 75, no. 4 (1996): 447–458. https://doi.org/10.3382/ps.0750447.

69 Schmutz, Jan B., Laurenz L. Meier, and Tanja Manser. "How Effective Is Teamwork Really? The Relationship Between Teamwork and Performance in Healthcare Teams: A Systematic Review and Meta-Analysis." *BMJ Open* 9 (2019): e028280. https://doi.org/10.1136/bmjopen-2018-028280.

70 Stojan, Jon. "The Importance of Cross-Departmental Collaboration in the Workplace and How You Can Foster It." *Forbes.* April 27, 2023. https://www.forbes.com.au/life/brand-voice/the-importance-of-cross-departmental-collaboration-in-the-workplace-and-how-you-can-foster-it/.

71 Bachrach, Daniel G., Benjamin C. Powell, Brian J. Collins, and R. Glenn Richey. "Effects of Task Interdependence on the Relationship Between Helping Behavior and Group Performance." *Journal of Applied Psychology* 91, no. 6 (2006): 1396–1405. https://doi.org/10.1037/0021-9010.91.6.1396.

Jolly, Phillip M., Dejun Tony Kong, and Kyoung Yong Kim. "Social Support at Work: An Integrative Review." *Journal of Organizational Behavior* 42, no.2 (2020): 229–251. https://doi.org/10.1002/job.2485.

Tai, Cheng-Ling. "The Relationships Among Leader Social Support, Team Social Support, Team Stressors and Team Performance." *Procedia-Social and Behavioral Sciences* 57, no. 9 (2012): 404–411. https://doi.org/10.1016/j.sbspro.2012.09.1204.

72 Davis, Walter D., Neal Mero, and Joseph M. Goodman. "The Interactive Effects of Goal Orientation and Accountability on Task Performance." *Human Performance* 20, no. 1 (2007): 1– 21. https://doi.org/10.1080/08959280709336926.

Kou, Chia-Yu and Virginia Stewart. "Group Accountability: A Review and Extension of Existing Research." *Small Group Research* 49, no. 1 (2017): 34–61. https://doi.org/10.1177/1046496417712.

Stewart, Virginia R., Deirdre G. Snyder, and Chia-Yu Kou. "We Hold Ourselves Accountable: A Relational View of Team Accountability." *Journal of Business Ethics* 183 (2023): 691–712. https://doi.org/10.1007/s10551-021-04969-z.

73 Morin, Amy. "Why New Year's Resolutions Set You Up to Fail." *Psychology Today.* December 29, 2024. https://www.psychologytoday.com/us/blog/what-mentally-strong-people-dont-do/202412/why-new-years-resolutions-set-you-up-to-fail.

74 Ito, Tim and Ryan Changcoco. "The Accountability Advantage." Association for Talent Development. December 2, 2019. https://www.td.org/content/td-magazine/the-accountability-advantage.

75 Gruenert, Steve and Todd Whitaker. *School Culture Rewired: How to Define, Assess, and Transform It.* ASCD, 2015.

76 Doran, George T. "There's a S.M.A.R.T. Way to Write Managements's Goals and Objectives." *Management Review* 70, no. 11 (1981): 35. https://openurl.ebsco.com/EPDB%3Agcd%3A12%3A32629916/detailv2?sid=ebsco%3Aplink%3Acrawler&id=ebsco%3Agcd%3A6043491&link_origin=www.google.com.

77 Locke, Edwin A. and Gary P. Latham. "Building a Practically Useful Theory of Goal Setting and Task Motivation: A 35-Year Odyssey." *American Psychologist* 57, no. 9 (2022): 705–717. https://doi.org/10.1037/0003-066X.57.9.705.

78 Broedling, Laurie and Vern Goodwalt. "Benefits of Using the Team Excellence Framework: How Your Teams and Organization Can Achieve Outstanding Improvements." *Journal for Quality and Participation* 35, no. 1 (2012): 20–25. https://search.proquest.com/openview/f6771e6858437535dac853dba32e20f8/1.

79 Grant, Adam. *Think Again: The Power of Knowing What You Don't Know.* Penguin, 2023.

80 Six Seconds. "2022 Workplace Vitality Report." 2022. https://www.6seconds.org/2022-workplace-vitality-report/.

81 Edmondson, Amy C. "Strategies for Learning from Failure." *Harvard Business Review*, April 2011. https://hbr.org/2011/04/strategies-for-learning-from-failure.

82 Di Stefano, Giada, Francesca Gino, Gary P. Pisano, and Bradley R. Staats. "Learning by Thinking: How Reflection Aids Performance." *SSRN Electronic Journal* 2015, no. 1 (2014). https://doi.org/10.2139/ssrn.2414478.

83 Tatel, Corey, Ben Wigert, and Sangeeta Agrawal. "The Top Four Reasons for Taking a New Job." Gallup. February 23, 2025. https://www.gallup.com/workplace/656906/top-four-reasons-taking-new-job.aspx.

84 Wigert, Ben and Corey Tatel. "The Great Detachment: Why Employees Feel Stuck." Gallup. December 2, 2024. https://www.gallup.com/workplace/653711/great-detachment-why-employees-feel-stuck.aspx.

85 Allan, Blake A., Cassondra Batz-Barbarich, Haley M. Sterling, and Louis Tay. "Outcomes of Meaningful Work: A Meta-Analysis." *Journal of Management Studies* 56, no. 3 (2018): 500–528. https://doi.org/10.1111/joms.12406.

Lysova, Evgenia I., Blake A. Allan, Bryan J. Dik, et al. "Fostering Meaningful Work in Organizations: A Multi-Level Review and

Integration." *Journal of Vocational Behavior* 110, part B (2019): 374–389. https://doi.org/10.1016/j.jvb.2018.07.004.

Van Wingerden, Jessica, and Joost Van der Stoep. "The Motivational Potential of Meaningful Work: Relationships with Strengths Use, Work Engagement, and Performance." *PloS One* 13, no. 6 (2018): e0197599. https://doi.org/10.1371/journal.pone.0197599.

86 Gartenberg, Claudine, Andrea Prat, and George Serafeim. "Corporate Purpose and Financial Performance." *Organization Science* 30, no. 1 (2016): 1–18. https://doi.org/10.1287/orsc.2018.1230.

Lynn, Gary and Faruk Kalay. "The Effect of Vision and Role Clarity on Team Performance." *Journal of Business Economics and Finance* 4, no. 3 (2015): 473. https://doi.org/10.17261/Pressacademia.2015313067.

Van Tuin, Lars, Wilmar B. Schaufeli, Anja Van den Broeck, and Willem van Rhenen. "A Corporate Purpose as an Antecedent to Employee Motivation and Work Engagement." *Frontiers in Psychology* 11 (2020). https://doi.org/10.3389/fpsyg.2020.572343.

87 Folkman, Joseph. "8 Ways to Ensure Your Vision Is Valued." *Forbes.* Last modified October 10, 2019. https://www.forbes.com/sites/joefolkman/2014/04/22/8-ways-to-ensure-your-vision-is-valued/.

88 Microsoft. "About Microsoft." Accessed June 5, 2025. https://www.microsoft.com/en-us/about.

89 Whole Foods Market. "Mission & Values." Accessed June 5, 2025. https://www.wholefoodsmarket.com/mission-values.

90 IKEA. "The IKEA Vision and Values". Accessed June 5, 2025. https://www.ikea.com/us/en/this-is-ikea/about-us/the-ikea-vision-and-values-pub9aa779d0/.

91 Finegan, Joan E. "The Impact of Person and Organizational Values on Organizational Commitment." *Journal of Occupational and Organizational Psychology* 73, no. 2 (2010): 149–169. https://doi.org/10.1348/096317900166958.

92 Jin, K. Gregory and Ronald G. Drozdenko. "Relationships Among Perceived Organizational Core Values, Corporate Social Responsibility, Ethics, and Organizational Performance Outcomes: An Empirical

Study of Information Technology Professionals." *Journal of Business Ethics* 92 (2010): 341–359. https://doi.org/10.1007/s10551-009-0158-1.

93 Qualtrics. "Employees Who Feel Aligned with Company Values Are More Likely to Stay." April 25, 2022. https://www.qualtrics.com/blog/company-values-employee-retention/.

94 Duckworth, Angela L., Christopher Peterson, Michael D. Matthews, and Dennis R. Kelly. "Grit: Perseverance and Passion for Long-Term Goals." *Journal of Personality and Social Psychology* 92, no. 6 (2007): 1087–1101. https://doi.org/10.1037/0022-3514.92.6.1087.

95 Schein, Edgar H. *Organizational Culture and Leadership.* 4th ed. Jossey-Bass, 2010.

96 Cameron, Kim S. and Robert E. Quinn. *Diagnosing and Changing Organizational Culture: Based on the Competing Values Framework.* 3rd ed. Jossey-Bass, 2011.

97 Center for Creative Leadership. "Visual Explorer® Facilitator Set, Letter Size (8.5in x 11in)." Accessed June 5, 2025. https://shop.ccl.org/usa/visual-explorer-facilitator-set-letter-size-8-5in-x-11in.html.

98 Grant, Adam M. 2008. "Employees Without a Cause: The Motivational Effects of Prosocial Impact in Public Service." *International Public Management Journal* 11, no. 1 (2008): 48–66. https://doi.org/10.1080/10967490801887905.

99 Allan, Blake A., Cassondra Batz-Barbarich, Haley M. Sterling, and Louis Tay. "Outcomes of Meaningful Work: A Meta-Analysis." *Journal of Management Studies* 56, no. 3 (2018): 500–528. https://doi.org/10.1111/joms.12406.

Fairlie, Paul. "Meaningful Work, Employee Engagement, and Other Key Employee Outcomes: Implications for Human Resource Development." *Advances in Developing Human Resources* 13, no. 4 (2011): 508–525. https://doi.org/10.1177/1523422311431679.

Reece, Andrew, David Yaden, Gabriella Kellerman, et al. "Mattering Is an Indicator of Organizational Health and Employee Success." *The Journal of Positive Psychology* 16, no. 2 (2021): 228–248. https://doi.org/10.1080/17439760.2019.1689416.

100 Office of the US Surgeon General. "The US Surgeon General's Framework for Workplace Mental Health & Well-Being." 2022. https://www.hhs.gov/sites/default/files/workplace-mental-health-well-being.pdf.

101 Mercurio, Zach. "How to Create Mattering at Work." Medium. November 15, 2022. https://zachmercurio.medium.com/how-to-create-mattering-at-work-bef6b78fbe40.

102 Anicich, Eric and Alice J. Lee. "Research: More Powerful People Express Less Gratitude." *Harvard Business Review.* April 25, 2022. https://hbr.org/2022/04/research-more-powerful-people-express-less-gratitude.

103 Achor, Shawn. *Big Potential: How Transforming the Pursuit of Success Raises Our Achievement, Happiness, and Well-Being.* Crown Currency, 2018.

104 Anicich, Eric and Alice J. Lee. "Research: More Powerful People Express Less Gratitude." *Harvard Business Review.* April 25, 2022. https://hbr.org/2022/04/research-more-powerful-people-express-less-gratitude.

Index